SFS✴100

A CENTURY *of* SERVICE

GEORGETOWN UNIVERSITY

Walsh School *of* Foreign Service

GEORGETOWN UNIVERSITY

PRINTED IN CHINA

Distributed by Georgetown University Press

First Edition

ISBN: 978-1-7332831-0-6 (Hardcover)
ISBN: 978-1-7332831-1-3 (Paperback)
ISBN: 978-1-7332831-2-0 (Digital)

Visit School of Foreign Service at www.sfs.georgetown.edu
Visit Washingtonian Custom Media at www.washingtoniancustommedia.com

Produced by
WASHINGTONIAN CUSTOM MEDIA
1828 L Street, NW, Suite 200, Washington, DC 20036

James Byles, President and Publisher • Paul O'Donnell, Writer
Ken DeCell, Editor • Michael Bessire, Design • Kelci Schuler, Photo Editor
Cathy Dobos, Rina Huang, George Perikles and Gloria Roh, Production Team

FOR GEORGETOWN UNIVERSITY EDMUND A. WALSH SCHOOL OF FOREIGN SERVICE

Joel S. Hellman, Dean of Georgetown Walsh School of Foreign Service
Will Layman, Executive Director of the Centennial
Jen Lennon, Director of Communications
Ara Friedman, Editorial Manager

A
CENTURY
of
SERVICE

Born in an hour that enriches it with a heritage
of dearly purchased lessons in the meaning of true citizenship
and pure patriotism, the School of Foreign Service hopefully
dedicates its future to the exemplification of the Christian trilogy;
to Law, that Justice may prevail in the economic and
political sciences; to Beauty, that she may not walk unnoticed
in the busy marts of trade, among the money changers,
and to Conscience, that sound Morality may ever guide our
beloved country and countrymen in all their dealings,
be they with nations or individuals.

———

FATHER EDMUND A. WALSH, S.J.

Contents

BEFORE FOGGY BOTTOM
Now the Old Executive Office Building, the State, War and Navy Building, beside the White House, was home to the Department of State from 1875 until the end of the Second World War.

By Madeleine Albright

WHEN THE SCHOOL OF FOREIGN SERVICE WAS BORN IN 1919, A WAR HAD JUST ended, and borders in Europe, the Middle East and Asia were being redrawn. Americans seated around dinner tables across the country and around the negotiating table at Versailles were engaged in robust debate about whether the United States' role in the world must change and how we might rise to the occasion if it did.

In a moment whose challenges were rivaled in magnitude only by its opportunities, America needed an institution that could effectively prepare young students to answer emergency calls to global service. Father Edmund A. Walsh recognized the lack of such programs in American higher education and, only two years after becoming Dean of Georgetown College, chose the college to host his prescient experiment.

BY THE MIDDLE OF THAT CENTURY, HOWEVER, NEW FORCES HAD emerged that threatened to destroy the nascent order to which Walsh and early students of the School of Foreign Service had devoted themselves.

Those forces that proved the urgency of Father Walsh's vision and sparked a second major world conflict are the same ones that drove my family from our home in Czechoslovakia, first when Hitler's army marched on Prague and again when the Communists came to power. After arriving in Denver, Colorado, my life, career, and family took me to various places across the United States and eventually to Washington, DC, for work as a legislative aide to Senator Ed Muskie and, later, as a National Security Council staffer in the Carter administration.

As much as I loved working in the White House, the 1981 change in administration ultimately brought me to the Edmund A. Walsh School of Foreign Service—funding had come through to support a new female faculty member, a practitioner, and thanks to the PhD in public law and government I had earned several years earlier, I fit the bill. Teaching at the SFS has been the most rewarding experience of my life, and I agreed to interrupt my professorship only so I could serve a 1968 graduate of the SFS whose time here would help propel him to this nation's highest office.

President William Jefferson Clinton's story is remarkable, but he is by no means the only distinguished graduate of this school. In every major sector and industry, Georgetown SFS graduates have contributed considerably to the formulation of the 21st-century world.

Consider, for instance, those such as J. Lane Kirkland (SFS'48), the celebrated labor leader who led the AFL-CIO for more than a decade and a half; George Tenet (SFS'76), whose time as head of Central Intelligence made him the second-longest serving director in that Agency's history; and Tessie San Martin

(SFS'80), whose leadership at the World Bank and Plan International has made the world a safer and healthier place to live.

Or other courageous women such as Paula Dobriansky (SFS'77), whose contributions to Ireland's peace process earned her a Distinguished Service Medal, the Department of State's highest honor, and Aimee Mullins (SFS'98), the fashion icon and track-and-field world-record holder who competed for and led the U.S. delegation to the 2012 London Paralympic Games.

Or others who walked the Hilltop at the same time, such as General John R. Allen (SSP'83), former Commander of the International Security Assistance Force in Afghanistan and current head of the Brookings Institution, and Nasser Judeh (SFS'83), former Minister of Foreign Affairs of Jordan when that country's partnership and leadership on key transnational issues was so vitally important.

The U.S. Congress of today would also not be the same without SFS alums, seven of whom were elected or reelected to positions in the House of Representatives in 2018.

And considering the impact of the SFS, I would be remiss not to mention a few of those whom I have taught personally —

PEACE PARTY
Opposite: Ambassador Paula Dobriansky (SFS '77) at a reception at Stormont Castle in Belfast with Northern Ireland Deputy First Minister Martin McGuinness, New York Mayor Michael Bloomberg, media executive Sir Anthony O'Reilly, and First Minister Ian Paisley.

"Teaching at the School of Foreign Service has been the most rewarding experience of my life, and I agreed to interrupt my professorship only so I could serve a 1968 graduate of the SFS whose time here would help propel him to this nation's highest office."

"We must remember that this school was not founded because its forefathers expected the world to be a simpler place to live in and lead. As long as there are wrongs in this world, there must also be those trained, and trained at the highest level, to right them."

like David Hale (SFS'83), Under Secretary of State for Political Affairs and former U.S. Ambassador to Jordan, Lebanon and Pakistan; his classmate Joe Cirincione (MSFS'83), who heads the Ploughshares Fund's efforts to reduce and eliminate the threat posed by nuclear weapons; and Taro Kono (SFS'86), Minister of Foreign Affairs of Japan, whose leadership has played a major role in opening his country to increased international investment and collaboration. Michael Sheehan (MSFS'88) worked for me at the United Nations several years after I taught him, and went on to become one of the world's leading counterterrorism experts before his untimely passing in 2018. That I considered each of them friends long after they left Georgetown attests to the strength of bonds forged at SFS.

One hundred years after the founding of the School, we again find ourselves in a period of dramatic uncertainty. Not since the invention of democratic institutions have their liberal underpinnings been so thoroughly challenged. I wish I had not felt compelled to write my most recent book, *Fascism: A Warning*, but the reemergence of a trend that should have

died with Mussolini demanded it. The movement of violently displaced populations across and within borders has reached levels never before seen. New technologies have sped up the flow of information and allowed unheard perspectives to be voiced — sometimes responsibly, other times not.

We must remember, however, that this school was not founded because its forefathers expected the world to become a simpler place to live and lead. Father Walsh predicted that in fact the opposite would be true; he was right, and the growing complexity of international affairs in the 21st century only attests to this institution's importance. As long as there are wrongs in this world, there must also be those trained, and trained at the highest level, to right them.

Since the turn of the century, I have watched the SFS curriculum expand to keep pace with the technology-driven evolution of international affairs. Students who so recently benefitted from the School's cutting-edge academic offerings have gone on to serve the world as government officials, business executives, and human-rights advocates, and in so many other capacities. In each country I visit, I encounter more of these extraordinary young alums; each time, the words of Robert Frost ring truer and truer: "When I was young my teachers were the old. ... Now when I am old my teachers are the young."

I am forever grateful for the opportunity to teach — and, more importantly, to learn — at a place whose graduates have made, and will continue to make, such profound contributions to our world.

With gratitude and admiration,
Madeleine K. Albright
Former U.S. Secretary of State; Mortara Endowed Distinguished Professor in the Practice of Diplomacy

Introduction

by Dean Joel S. Hellman

A GLOBAL CONFLICT WREAKED DEVASTATION ON MULTIPLE CONTINENTS. ALMOST TEN MILLION combatants were dead and another seven million civilians perished. The leaders of the world gathered together with a mission no less ambitious than to end all war. They redrew national boundaries and remade empires. They recognized that enhanced trade and finance would bind nations together. They proposed new principles and institutions to secure peace. They rejected the balance of power politics that had dominated the previous century and committed to multilateralism and collective security as a new foundation for international affairs.

This was 1919. This was the world into which the very first U.S. school of international affairs would be born. Or, truly, into which it would be drafted for service.

For all of the war's horrors, its conclusion created a hunger for idealism. The Allied Powers met in Paris not only to sign the treaties that would end the war but to conceive of a new world order that could prevent such tragedy. President Woodrow Wilson and prime ministers David Lloyd George, Georges Clemenceau and Vittorio Orlando led delegations from 27 countries to attempt to reimagine global order and cooperation. The ambition of this effort was matched, perhaps, by its short-term futility.

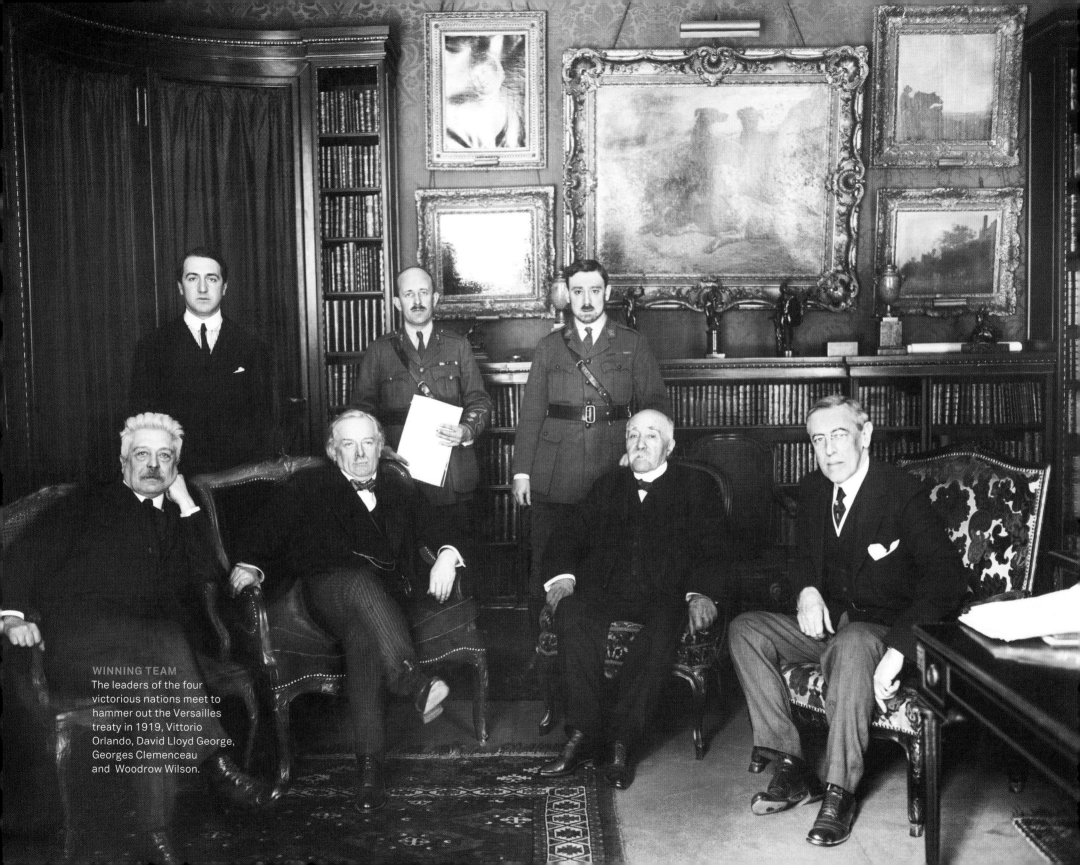

WINNING TEAM
The leaders of the four victorious nations meet to hammer out the Versailles treaty in 1919, Vittorio Orlando, David Lloyd George, Georges Clemenceau and Woodrow Wilson.

That ambition would focus on the United States, the nation that in so many ways had brought the Allied Powers to victory. The war transformed the United States from an inwardly focused power to a global superpower. The U.S. had been not only a critical military force in winning the war, but the effort's crucial financier. From the world's largest debtor nation, the U.S. emerged from the war as the world's largest creditor and, through its burgeoning exports, an economic and financial titan. The U.S. would take a new, critical place on the global stage.

It was in this context that a group of visionary Americans began to see the need for — and the opportunity in — creating a group of young people who would be trained to support and lead the nation's new role. They would pursue a globally oriented liberal arts education that would, as the first mission statement of the school suggested, "promote peace through understanding." They would seek to understand cultures by pursuing a multidisciplinary approach to mastery of language, history, politics and economics. They would emphasize the critical role that commerce and trade could play in securing peace. But most importantly, they would breed in a new generation of leaders a commitment of service to the world.

Georgetown was a natural home for a school of foreign service. It was a school with a proud liberal arts tradition, educating young men in a wide array of disciplines, while also a Jesuit university, committed to fostering a sense of mission in its students shaped by the Jesuits' dedication to serving the most vulnerable. And, of course, it was in Washington, DC — a city that would itself shape world affairs.

So the idea took root. The concept was proposed by Constantine McGuire, an economist who had been trained both at Harvard and in Paris and who served on the Inter-American High Commission dedicated to expanding commerce with

"Our mission and purpose — to prepare global leaders in service to the world through a multidisciplinary liberal arts education that marries theory and practice—is newly critical."

America's neighbors. For funding, he approached James A. Farrell, the president of U.S. Steel, which would play a leading role in America's global economic dominance by becoming the world's first company worth one billion dollars. Farrell, a self-made man and son of a ship captain who rose from sales clerk to CEO, would not only offer $20,000 to endow the new school but would become a School of Foreign Service professor, teaching classes on international trade until the end of his life.

Through the Catholic network, McGuire and Farrell would ultimately approach Georgetown's President, Father John B. Creeden, to find a home for this new school. Father Creeden, after initial hesitation, accepted the challenge and turned to Father Edmund A. Walsh to usher the school into existence. Father Walsh had been running Georgetown's program with the Student Army Training Corps, which educated officers in languages before sending them overseas. The new school of foreign service would significantly widen that mandate.

At the 75th anniversary of the SFS, Professor Seth P. Tillman wrote an elegant, two-volume history of the school itself, one volume devoted to the history of the institution and another focused on some of SFS's finest professors — the legendary teachers who carried out the work first imagined by McGuire, Farrell, Walsh and others.

FOCUS ON THE FUTURE 1953
Student studying at the administrative offices of the School of Foreign Service in Healy Hall.

This book tells a broader story. SFS was created for a mission. As Father Walsh said in his speech inaugurating the school: "Having been unprepared for war, we have highly resolved that we shall not be unprepared for peace." SFS was established to send its graduates overseas to make the world a better, safer, more prosperous place. Its story, then, must necessarily be the story of its impact on the world.

That is the story told by this book.

There are stories you will expect to find here of presidents and kings, of secretaries of state and diplomats. These are critical parts of the SFS story, the story of how the promise to train young people to solve problems across borders would succeed at the highest levels. Diplomacy figures prominently in these tales. Even today, SFS remains the largest feeder school for the U.S. Foreign Service.

But it is equally important that this book tell the stories that are out of the limelight but integral to achieving long- lasting policy change. Indeed, we know that most SFS graduates do not go on to become presidents or diplomats. The founders of SFS understood that the future peace and prosperity would rest not only on diplomacy but on trade, commerce, law, development and culture at all levels. And SFS faculty and graduates have played important roles in these areas and more. For SFS, foreign service was always more than preparation for the U.S. Foreign Service (which, incidentally was created five years after the SFS).

In these pages, you can follow the stories of SFS alumni and professors who had a critical impact in so many areas of global service. You can also trace some of the ideas of our alumni and faculty that shaped the debates and outcomes of key aspects of the global order over the past century. You will see strong trends over the decades.

The earliest graduates were heavily involved in trade and diplomacy. SFS graduates were in high demand during the expansion of world trade during the 1920s. Many would immediately go abroad to serve as commercial attachés in embassies all over the world. Many would go directly into trading and shipping. Indeed, shipping was a popular major during the first decade of the school and the initial requirement for admission to study shipping at SFS was one year of service at sea.

With the creation of the U.S. Foreign Service by the Rogers Act of 1924 and the decline of foreign trade as a result of the Great Depression, the SFS started to play a critical role in shaping the U.S. diplomatic corps. The SFS quickly became the largest feeder school into the State Department. Over time, the impact of SFS on U.S. diplomacy through its ambassadorial corps, career Foreign Service Officers and senior officials in U.S. foreign policymaking would be unparalleled. SFS would also come to have an unusually large share of representatives in the legislative and executive branches around the world, as well as multilateral institutions, shaping policy and connecting nations of the world.

SFS graduates have been no less important in other areas addressed by this book. During the war years, SFS graduates began to take leadership positions in national security, national defense and intelligence, a trend that remains to this day, nurtured by our world-class Security Studies Program. But we also trace the impact of our alumni in humanitarian work, in the arts, in journalism, in finance and in the law. The stories are occasionally well known, but more often they are the stories of lesser celebrated heroes who were inspired by their education and the ideals of our school to make a difference in the world. Who would have known that an early recipient of the Master of Science in Foreign Service (MSFS) degree and World War I veteran Laurence Stallings would go on to be a playwright, screenwriter, lyricist, literary critic, journalist, novelist and photographer whose autobiographical novel, *Plumes*, would be adapted in the King Vidor film *The Big*

Parade, MGM's largest grossing movie until *Gone With the Wind*?

Perhaps more important than any single career path, SFS can be proudest of the impact it has had on the role of women in international affairs. Having admitted women more than two decades before most of our peers (albeit for the first few years, only in the evening program), SFS saw its graduates go on to become the first female ambassadors in the Foreign Service. Two SFS women became presidents of their countries. And SFS faculty like Madeleine Albright and Jeane Kirkpatrick became pioneers in the study and practice of international affairs.

In collecting the stories of how SFS graduates and faculty have left their mark on world affairs, we see how the SFS lived up to its founding mission over the course of a century to establish a new cadre of leaders in service to the world. In demonstrating the range and breadth of areas that SFS alumni have influenced, we can see the impact of the school's commitment to a globally focused liberal arts education, which prepared students for such a wide range of career paths. And in showing the global reach of the SFS community, we can see the impact of the school's embrace of an internationally diverse student body which ultimately established an unparalleled network of international alumni committed to the core values of multilateralism and global engagement that motivated the school's founding.

A century after the end of World War I, the world again seems to be at an inflection point.

Many of the values that motivated the creation of the school are being challenged in the U.S. and many countries around the world: trade agreements, alliances, diplomatic norms and multilateral institutions. At the same time, extraordinary new challenges — the likes of which Woodrow Wilson, David Lloyd George and Father Walsh could hardly have imagined — are upon us. New technologies, like artificial intelligence and bioengineer-

ing, are transforming the security landscape, creating unprecedented new risks. Climate change threatens to remake the map of the modern world. New forms of communication are reshaping who can impact global affairs. Economic and financial interdependence are redefining global value chains, financial flows and labor mobility that test the significance of national borders.

And this is why the need for a school like SFS is just as urgent in 2019 as in 1919. Our mission and purpose — to prepare global leaders in service to the world through a multidisciplinary liberal arts education that marries theory and practice — is newly critical.

SFS is evolving to face the newest problems. Science and technology, culture and communications, business, and international development strategy are now subjects taught alongside economics, political science, languages and history. In a new century facing new problems, we embrace timeless values while investing in new skills and new ideas that reflect an ever-changing set of global challenges.

The story of SFS's next 100 years will be written eventually. Like the stories in this book, it will be that of people and ideas — but we know that the decisions we make today will be the foundation of those new stories of impact. And we know that future alumni, the remarkable people who will star in our school's second century, will have been drawn to SFS in part because of our remarkable history.

It is to those future heroes that this book is dedicated. This is the story of our century of service to the world. Your century is waiting for you. The tools for making a positive impact on that century will surely be learned right here at Georgetown.

Warm regards,

Joel S. Hellman

Dean, Georgetown Walsh School of Foreign Service

NOV, 1918
The United States and other Allied powers sign the Armistice that ends the First World War.

1919
Father Walsh founds the SFS.

1920
A group of 18 SFS students conduct an economic survey of Venezuela. The trip is funded by scholarship funds provided by the School. Walter J. Donnelly, a student who participated in the tour, later became the United States Ambassador to Venezuela.

1922
First Master of Science in Foreign Service students graduate. Obtaining a Master's in Foreign Service is described as: "A Master's degree may be obtained by taking a third year of advanced work on selected subjects, provided the Bachelor's degree has already been obtained."

1918
Constantine McGuire, a highly private expert on international trade, shops his idea for a specialized school of foreign relations to several U.S. universities. Georgetown University President John B. Creeden asks Father Edmund A. Walsh, S.J. to take on the project. Between 1919 and 1922, McGuire served as the SFS' unofficial executive secretary. Arguably his most significant contribution to the School's history came when he successfully convinced the president of U.S. Steel, James A. Farrell, to make an initial contribution of $20,000 toward a permanent endowment.

DEC, 1918
Memorandum circulated within the University discussing conception of the school.

1921
First class graduates, including many veterans of World War One and other older students.

1924
Rogers Act of 1924 establishes the Foreign Service of the United States within the State Department.

1926
First daytime classes established in SFS in the fall.

1932
The School of Foreign Service moves to Healy Hall.

1945
Father Walsh acts as a consultant to Justice Robert Jackson, the U.S. prosecutor at the Nuremberg Trials. Walsh conducted an informal interview with Major General Karl Haushofer, who had acted as a major academic influence on Hitler and Nazi ideology, to ascertain whether he ought to stand trial for war crimes. Walsh concluded that the actions of Haushofer did not meet the standard for prosecution.

1934
Anthony Kenkel (SFS'23) negotiates the first reciprocal trade agreement between Cuba and the United States, which dropped sugar tariffs from $2/pound to less than 1 cent/pound. Following World War II, Kenkel served on the U.S. delegation for the General Agreement of Tariffs and Trade, which laid the foundation for the World Trade Organization.

1945
Leon Dostert (SFS'31) pioneers a system of simultaneous translation at the Nuremberg Trials. A system based on Dostert's invention continues to be used to this day at the United Nations. Later, Dostert was instrumental in the foundation of the SFS' Institute of Language and Linguistics, of which he served as the first Dean.

1946
Anne S. Lawrence and Mary Alice Sheridan become the first two women to graduate from the SFS.

1949-52
Richard Butrick (SFS'21) serves as Director of the Foreign Service during these critical early years of the Cold War.

1953
SFS starts admitting women as full-time day students.

1956
SFS' first graduate Willard Beaulac (SFS'21) is appointed as United States Ambassador to Argentina. Formerly he served in consular roles at missions in Mexico, Honduras, Nicaragua, Haiti, and Chile before the age of 30. Prior to Argentina, Beaulac was ambassador to Paraguay, Colombia, and was one of the last Americans to serve in that post to Cuba, before the severing of diplomatic relations between the two countries.

1949
Father Walsh opens the Institute of Languages and Linguistics within the SFS.

1954
Professor Jan Karski begins teaching at Georgetown, where he taught until 1984. Karski had made his name as a Polish resistance fighter and spy during the years of Nazi occupation in World War II. He provided eyewitness accounts of the Holocaust to Allied leaders, including President Roosevelt.

1958
The school is renamed after Father Walsh and the school's building on the eastern part of campus is dedicated in his name, in a ceremony attended by President Dwight D. Eisenhower.

1959
The Center for Eurasian, Russian and East European Studies was founded in order to prepare students for a career in foreign service during the Cold War.

1969
SFS drops its quota of no more than one female per eight males that was begun in 1954.

1959
The Center for Latin American Studies is founded. It was originally named the Georgetown University Latin American Studies Program, until the name was changed in 1990.

1967
Jeane Kirkpatrick joins the faculty in the government department. In 1981, she became the Ambassador to the United Nations in the administration of President Ronald Reagan. Following her tenure as Ambassador, Kirkpatrick returned to teaching at Georgetown in 1986.

1970
Peter F. Krogh becomes Dean of the School of Foreign Service at the age of 32. He is often remembered as the "second founder" of the School of Foreign Service for the reforms enacted during his tenure. Krogh successfully healed divisions among faculty, and ensured the SFS would continue to have a separate teaching staff. In addition, he revised the curriculum, allowing for more electives. Krogh served as dean until 1995.

1975
The Center for Contemporary Arab Studies is established. Today the center uses its expert faculty to put on more than 100 Arab-world related courses for Georgetown students, while at the same time producing groundbreaking research.

1977

Henry Kissinger becomes an SFS professor after President Ford loses reelection. Kissinger had served as Secretary of State between 1972 and 1977, and National Security Advisor from 1969 to 1975. At Georgetown, Kissinger regales students with tales of his negotiations with Chairman Mao.

1978

The Institute for the Study of Diplomacy is founded. The institute seeks to better understand the nexus of theory and practice, and to enhance and expand an appreciation of the role of diplomacy as a critical tool in national policy.

1980

The African Studies Program is established. The program aims to maintain and expand its comparative advantage in research and teaching through an emphasis on a foundation of understanding Africa's peoples, cultures and languages.

1979

The Landegger Program in International Business Diplomacy is founded to train students for work at the intersection of international public and private sector activities. The first graduate students to obtain a certificate graduate in 1980.

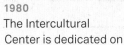

1980

The Intercultural Center is dedicated on September 24, 1980.

1980

The Asian Studies Program is founded. The program, which offers both undergraduate courses and a graduate degree, recognizes the importance of Asia as a home to over half the global population, and many of the largest and fastest-growing economies, as well as some of the most dangerous regimes in the world.

TIMELINE

1982
Charles Pirtle arrives at Georgetown University as a professor in the School of Foreign Service. He is the creator of the legendary class Map of the Modern World, which has been a staple of alumni nostalgia ever since.

1990
The BMW Center for German and European Studies is founded, following the fall of the Berlin Wall.

1992
William Jefferson Clinton (SFS'68) wins the U.S. Presidential election. He enters the White House in 1993 and serves two terms.

1982
Madeleine Albright begins teaching at the School as an expert in Eastern Europe. Albright would later serve as President Clinton's Ambassador to the United Nations, and then Secretary of State before returning to teach at Georgetown.

1983
The first student with a certificate in Science, Technology and International Affairs (STIA) graduates. The major subsequently developed out of a certificate within the International Politics major, propelled by the Cold War and associated anti-nuclear protests, as well as increased awareness of the vanishing ozone layer and other environmental concerns. STIA becomes a major in the undergraduate program in the early 1990s.

1993
The Prince Alwaleed Bin Talal Center for Muslim-Christian Understanding is founded as the Center for Muslim-Christian Understanding. In 2005, HRH Prince Alwaleed Bin Talal donated $20 million to expand the work of the Center, which was renamed in his honor.

1994
The North American Free Trade Agreement comes into force. Andrew Shoyer (MSFS'86) is the principal U.S. legal counsel in the negotiation of market access rules of the treaty.

1995
The School of Foreign Service opens the Center for Australian, New Zealand & Pacific Studies, thanks to funding from the governments of Australia and New Zealand.

1996
George Tenet (SFS'76) becomes Director of the Central Intelligence Agency, having formerly served as the Deputy Director. Tenet is the second youngest director in history.

2003
The Center for Jewish Civilization, originally the Program for Jewish Civilization, is established.

1995
The National Security Studies Program (NSSP) is founded in 1977 as a certificate program associated with the Master of Arts in the Department of Government, and classes were held in the Pentagon. Founder and NSSP Director Dr. Stephen Gibert conceived the program as a "defense MBA," a concentrated, specialized course of study in defense analysis. In 1984, the program officially became the Master of Arts in National Security Studies, and in 1994, the NSSP discontinued all courses at the Pentagon and expanded its offerings on the University's main campus. In 1995, as part of the University's overall reorganization, it incorporated the SSP into the School of Foreign Service. The Center for Security Studies (CSS), which houses the Security Studies Master's Program was created in 2000.

1998
The Institute for the Study of International Migration is founded. It is an innovative multidisciplinary center that studies the social, economic, environmental, and political dimensions of international migration.

2000
Ruth Hansen (MSFS'70) is appointed director of the State Department Policy Planning and Coordination office. Prior to this she served as a political officer across the Balkans and deputy director of peacekeeping and humanitarian affairs. Previously, Hansen was told after failing her Foreign Service exam that she was going to Georgetown for grad school and that she'd probably marry a nice man and not have to worry about a career. In fact, she ended up having a 30-year State Department career.

2003
The Mortara Center for International Studies is established to advance scholarship and inform policy by combining the knowledge of scholars and the experience of international affairs practitioners to illuminate the essential factors that shape international relations. In 2005, it moves to the historic townhouse at 3600 N Street, NW where it continues to exist.

2005

The School of Foreign Service opens its campus in Education City, Qatar, in partnership with the Qatar Foundation. In 2015, the name was changed from Georgetown University School of Foreign Service in Qatar to Georgetown University in Qatar, to reflect its wider scope.

2010

Carol Lancaster (SFS'64) becomes the first female Dean of the School of Foreign Service. Lancaster came to SFS as a first-generation college student, and, after graduating in 1964, she went on to pursue a Fulbright scholarship in Bolivia before earning her Ph.D. at the London School of Economics and Political Science. She served in the U.S. Department of State's policy planning staff and as Deputy Assistant Secretary of State for Africa until she was selected as the first female Deputy Administrator for USAID, where she broke glass ceilings all over the world through her work in international development. She returned to SFS in 1996, where she worked as a professor until becoming Dean of the school from 2010 until her death in 2014.

2011

The Georgetown Institute for Women, Peace and Security is launched by then-Secretary of State Hillary Clinton, who continues to act as the Institute's honorary founding chair.

2012

The Global Human Development Program is founded. The goal of the Master of Global Human Development is to prepare students to understand the challenges of development and provide them with the tools and experience to address those challenges as successful professionals.

2019

The Center for Security and Emerging Technology (CSET) is established as a research organization focused on studying the security impacts of emerging technologies, supporting academic work in security and technology studies, and delivering nonpartisan analysis to the policy community. CSET aims to prepare a generation of policymakers, analysts, and diplomats to address the challenges and opportunities of emerging technologies. During its first two years, CSET will focus on the effects of progress in artificial intelligence and advanced computing.

Chapter One

The Beginnings

O N FEBRUARY 11, 1920, AT THE NEW EBBITT HOTEL AT 14th and F Streets in downtown Washington, DC, 15 members of the Delta Phi Epsilon fraternity and their honored guests attended an "Enitiatory Dinner," the first formal meeting of an organization founded a few weeks earlier in the basement of the Catholic Community Center on E Street, Northwest, for students at Georgetown University's School of Foreign Service, itself barely a year old.

Packed snugly into a paneled dining room at the Ebbitt — not the current Old Ebbitt Grill located near the same spot, but a Second Empire building that resembled a white wedding cake and was torn down in the 1920s — the Delta Phi founders dined at round tables laid with white linen and heavy silver and offered toasts to the school's cofounder and regent, the Reverend Edmund A. Walsh. They heard speeches from Congressman Clay S. Briggs, a Texas Democrat and a member of the House Ways and Means Committee.

Wrapped in dark suits and high collars, most were older than the first- and second-year students at today's School of Foreign Service. Many had fought in the world war that had ended with the signing of the Versailles Treaty in Paris seven months before and were ready to get on with their careers. The new school's courses were taught in the evening, convenient for men who were hoping to complete an education they had begun in their daytime jobs in U.S. government agencies, most dealing with transportation and trade.

FOUNDING FATHER
Father Edmund A. Walsh at Georgetown (left); the Enitiatory Dinner of Delta Phi Epsilon fraternity at the Ebbitt Hotel on February 21, 1920. Walsh is in the back row second from the left (right).

DELTA PHI EPSILON HEADQUARTERS
The lease for Delta Phi Epsilon's first house. The guarantor was
School of Foreign Service cofounder Constantine E. McGuire.

**GEORGETOWN
FROM ABOVE**
A 1918 aerial view of
Georgetown University.

Most of all, they were eager to take advantage of their country's unprecedented business opportunities abroad.

On the front pages of the newspapers, in popular songs and in political rhetoric, the recent war in Europe had been won by the late surge of American doughboys arriving on the Western front, tilting the balance in the trench-bound stalemate toward the Allies. Anyone who read the financial pages knew that this was only a small part of the United States' saving role: Great Britain, France and Italy had only been able to survive to see the victory — and to force the Central Powers to surrender — thanks to an enormous influx of American cash. By war's close, the European powers owed the American taxpayer almost $10 billion, or roughly $100 billion in current dollars.

These balance sheets were far outweighed by the huge disparity in wealth between Europe and the United States. It is estimated that at the war's conclusion the United States' national wealth, at nearly $400 billion, was more than triple that of France, and more than the three richest European countries' wealth combined.

In November of 1919, Georgetown's President John Creeden had invited Adolph Miller, a governor of the then six-year-old Federal Reserve Board, to help celebrate the founding of the School of Foreign Service. Miller's speech to the university faculty and students captures the sense of sheer astonishment the country's leaders felt at the promise of America's financial position. "From being a country which has borrowed from the older nations of Europe for the purpose of developing our internal resources, for building our railways, for constructing factories and which was debtor to the extent of almost half a billion dollars a year," Miller said, " ... we have become a creditor country even to the richest of the nations of the Old World." The $5-billion loan made to support England and France in 1915 was the subject

"An inhabitant of London could order by telephone, sipping his morning tea in bed, the various products of the whole earth in such quantity as he might see fit, and reasonably expect their early delivery upon his doorstep."
— JOHN MAYNARD KEYNES

of three months of negotiations with the two European powers. When it was done, Miller recalled, "[it] was the first clear indication that the war brought with it of how strong we were financially and economically, how much stronger we were than we had ever even in our most boastful moments thought."

What Miller didn't mention was that in relying on Wall Street loans to pay for the war, London had effectively relinquished its place as the capital of international finance to New York.

If America's situation was good, its prospects were even brighter. Before the war the British had enjoyed an unrivaled command of the seas, both militarily in their legendary Royal Navy and in its dominant cargo fleet. But the demands of the war had tied up Britain's merchant ships — in part with transporting American troops to Europe — while the United States had carried on a brisk trade with Latin America and Japan. American ships also streamed across the Atlantic to feed Europeans whose fields had been despoiled by four years of grinding combat. The needs of the world as it slowly reconstructed economies after the war fed a postwar expansion in American industry. When the School of Foreign Service held its first classes in February of

1919, the United States was poised to surpass the United Kingdom as the world's leading exporter.

In his critical report from the Paris peace conference, *"The Economic Consequences of the Peace,"* the legendary British economist John Maynard Keynes wrote that before the disruptions of World War I, "[a]n inhabitant of London could order by telephone, sipping his morning tea in bed, the various products of the whole earth in such quantity as he might see fit, and reasonably expect their early delivery upon his doorstep."

If consumers were enjoying the first blushes of what we'd now call globalization, business had undergone its own global revolution. A British merchant, Keynes continued, "could at the same moment and by the same means adventure his wealth in the natural resources and new enterprises of any quarter of the world, and share, without exertion or even trouble, in their prospective fruits and advantages."

Now, with the war over, the new and rapidly expanding center of that world economy was the United States. Suddenly, standing in the place of Keynes's Londoner was the American businessman.

Americans "were intrigued by globalization," says Marc Busch, the Karl F. Landegger Professor of International Business Diplomacy at the School of Foreign Service. "There was the idea that no market was too distant, or too remote."

American business leaders were anxious to capitalize on the United States' new place in the world economy. One of the most visible proponents of globalization was James A. Farrell, the president of the U.S. Steel Corporation. Known in later years as the "Dean of Foreign Trade" for his promotion of American products overseas, particularly steel, Farrell was avid to pursue business abroad for U.S. Steel and its fellow manufacturers; even prior to the outbreak of war in Europe, he had founded an organization called the National Foreign Trade Council and

set himself up as chairman. He also served as chairman of the foreign relations committee of the United States Chamber of Commerce and was a member of the Pan American Society.

It was most likely in these circles that he met Constantine McGuire, an economist and financial consultant who had trained at Harvard and, before the war, at the French government's École Des Langues Orientales Vivantes in Paris. Like Farrell, McGuire was a devout Catholic and well-connected supporter of church causes; though McGuire was always careful to protect his privacy and that of his clients, he is said to have advised the Vatican on financial matters.

McGuire had spent much of the war in Washington as the assistant to the Secretary-General of the International High Commission, a Treasury Department agency delegated to carry out the aims of the Pan American Financial Conference of 1915, with "a view to bringing about uniformity in the commercial laws of different countries," in the description of a contemporary chronicle. But from this perch McGuire had seen the opportunity the war afforded the United States, and by 1917 he had drawn up a plan for a school of diplomacy and trade.

"What I had had in mind was the intensive study of those factors which determine the course of foreign policy," he later wrote. The range of studies should be carefully focused on the policy-making and long-ranged aspects of international relations. An essential component of his scheme was to give students "special auxiliary training in languages." It would be the first such school of its kind in the United States.

Like the chiefs of U.S. corporations, there were many at the U.S. Department of Commerce who were interested in the development of such an academy. In October of 1919, Roy MacElwee, who headed the department's Bureau of Foreign and Domestic Commerce, published a "bulletin" titled *Train-*

PIECES IN PLACE
The school's first classroom building on E Street NW (right).

ing for Foreign Trade. MacElwee's 200-page volume, with an approving forward by President Wilson's Commerce Secretary, William Cox Redfield, laid out the necessity for a school like the one McGuire had in mind. "A country may have goods that are needed abroad, it may have ships in which to carry them, it may have adequate banking and facilities," MacElwee wrote, "but unless it has a trained personnel its foreign trade operations will be unduly costly and irritating."

Despite the obvious necessity for his school, McGuire at first had trouble convincing a university to host his project. Georgetown history professor Carroll Quigley later surmised, in a biographical article about McGuire, that the school would have gone to Harvard had it not refused McGuire a faculty position in Cambridge years earlier because of an unwritten rule against hiring Catholics to teach medieval history. Instead McGuire took his plan first to Father Thomas Gasson, then Dean of the Georgetown University Graduate School, and Georgetown's president, Father John Creeden.

"Father Creeden could not see his way clear to take it on," McGuire wrote in a letter years afterward. "I then tried to interest Bishop Thomas J. Shahan, of the Catholic University, who likewise felt it beyond his resources."

But in summer of 1918, McGuire discussed his plan for the school with Father Richard Tierney, the editor of the Jesuit magazine *America.* The bluff, opinionated Tierney, who was interested in Catholic Ireland's rebellion against Great Britain and anti-clericalism in Mexico, was in the middle of transforming the magazine into a forum that reflected his personality and interests. "The next day he told me that Father Creeden would receive me the following Sunday so as to discuss it once more," McGuire wrote. "It was then accepted in principle; and when the armistice came, the plan was given effect.

WORLD VIEWS
From the beginning, the School of Foreign Service offered resources, from language training to geographical materials, to open the world to its graduates. Students, shown here in 1953, examine maps in the SFS Geographic Library.

Father Edmund Walsh, who for the previous two years had overseen Georgetown's work with the Student Army Training Corps — an intensive language course for officers going overseas — was assigned to build on McGuire's plan.

The school was launched on February 17, 1919, with 70 students and 17 professors. In August, Farrell announced the establishment of a fund to endow the school with a half-million dollars; he opened up the subscriptions with $20,000 of his own. In October, the first regular semester started with 300 students and a staff of 33 professors — many of them drafted by McGuire.

The men gathered at the New Ebbitt four months later had a particularly good view of the United States' ballooning trade. Most of those enrolled in the new school, whose classes were at first held after working hours, had day jobs at the Commerce Department. At the speaker's table, in fact, sat a man whom many of the students called their boss — Roy MacElwee, who had been an evangelist for Walsh and McGuire's nascent school, advising the best and brightest of his employees to enroll at Georgetown to get an inside track on understanding markets abroad.

MacElwee's faith in the school was rewarded when he was made dean of the School of Foreign Service in June of 1920.

By that time the new Republican president, Warren G. Harding, had replaced the Democrat Redfield with Herbert Hoover, by far the most celebrated Commerce Secretary then or since. A millionaire mining engineer and executive, Hoover had come out of the war a hero twice over — first for organizing the evacuation of 120,000 American citizens caught in Europe at the outbreak of the war, then for saving Belgium from a food crisis that followed the German invasion of the country. Hoover, who had toyed with a presidential run himself, now set about transforming Commerce from a sleepy department charged with overseeing the census, the geographical survey and the

lighthouse service into a boosterish Chamber of Commerce for the American century — what William Leach called in his 1993 history, *Land of Desire*, "a bulging databank for businessmen."

The chief instrument of Hoover's promotion campaign was MacElwee's former bureau. Hoover appointed as the new director Julius Klein, a Harvard economic historian who turned the bureau into a public-relations machine as much for Hoover as for American merchants. While touting major corporations, Klein was careful to promote anyone who wanted to play in the newly opened field of international trade. His annual reports to Hoover were bursting with big and small victories. "A large southern textile mill made its first foreign connection through the bureau, resulting in sales of about $80,000 worth of goods in the past eight months," boasted the 1922 report, which included encomiums from the companies served. "We much appreciate the service rendered and believe there is no other Government that supplies such information," wrote a New York textile manufacturer.

These results found their way into the newspapers, and if businessmen didn't encounter the bureau's name there, they might read about it in one of the agency's brochures. "Now the

"With tariffs uniformly high, the debate over trade diplomacy focused on the concept of reciprocity — the practice of lowering duties on imports coming from certain trading partners, or 'more favored nations,' in return for the same preferential treatment. The key advocate for reciprocity was a visionary School of Foreign Service professor named William Smith Culbertson."

little man, like the big man, is a unit in the national manufacturing, exporting and selling scheme," read one pamphlet, "and the Department of Commerce is his sales organization."

Under MacElwee's influence — or Klein's, or both — a School of Foreign Service degree quickly became a necessary credential for success. In 1921, the school graduated the chief of the bureau's Foreign Service division, Harold Dotter, and his classmate Harold Gruber, who ran the bureau's Commercial Intelligence division. David S. Green was already serving as assistant chief of the bureau's Western European Division when he got his Bachelor's of Foreign Service degree in 1922.

Many in the early classes didn't stay long enough to get their diplomas. "Unfortunately, the School of Foreign Service will have fewer by far graduates than had been expected because after one year's work many of the students have been called to interesting and responsible positions by private firms and for the Government," wrote MacElwee in the journal "The World's Markets" in March of 1921. "In the Bureau of Foreign and Domestic Commerce alone, the Trade Commissioner in Tokyo, the Secretary to the Commercial Attache in Tokyo, the Secretary to the Commissioner in Zurich and several others have already gone overseas."

Businesses were equally avid for the new foreign-service recruits. Dean MacElwee told the story of one firm that took 12 graduates as trainees in its Latin American office and was so pleased with them that it asked a few months later for 40 more, a request that was denied "because such a large number of the first class would almost break up the school."

Wherever they latched on, the game was to build networks, seek out opportunities to make deals, and expand America's reach. "The job was to establish business contacts," says Professor Busch. "It's trying to find the guy on the ground who can get you into the new market."

Equally important was explaining the rules of the new markets to the home office once trade had been established. This was especially true of Asian countries that newly beckoned American suppliers. Japan, not counted in the top 10 before the war, had by the early 1920s become the world's fourth-largest trading nation. Representing U.S. interests in Tokyo was Halleck Butts, reportedly the youngest person to be made a trade commissioner — an assignment announced at a Delta Phi Epsilon dinner in the spring of 1920.

Butts's reports home capture the range of knowledge that his countrymen were looking for. Besides discussing a slump in the Japanese silk trade and the effect of silver prices on China's purchasing power, Butts passed along crucial tips about local customs. Merchants in Yokohama's harbor, he said, have two methods of taking delivery of goods — "the one over the pier, the other over ship's side" to barges waiting below. For this reason, Butts warned, "Japanese importer considers advance notice of a shipment to be of prime importance."

Hoover and Klein had a particular interest in Latin America. As trade rebounded after the war, Germany and other European nations moved to reestablish trade with South American countries. The United States, standing on an economic version of the Monroe Doctrine, looked to maintain its position as South America's primary trading partner. (Klein, who had taught Latin American economic history at Harvard, was chief of the Bureau of Foreign and Domestic Commerce's Latin American Division and served as commercial attache in Buenos Aires before being promoted to director.)

The importance of South American trade is evident in the number of early SFS graduates who began their careers in Mexico, Chile, Argentina and Peru. In 1924, the Republic of Argentina approached Hoover's department looking for help with raising

GOVERNMENT MAN
Roy MacElwee, most likely at his desk at the Commerce Department, about the time he became dean of the School of Foreign Service.

CLASS PORTRAIT
The SFS student body, pictured in the 1920 Domesday Booke.

> "Kenkel (SFS'24), who had been meeting with the Cubans since 1927, now made a deal that reduced tariffs on sugar exports from $2 per pound to under a penny. In return, Cuba would take more American goods. From 1933 to 1935, exports to Cuba increased 140 percent."

and exporting cotton. A worldwide boom had led several Latin American countries to pursue production of "el oro blanco." Hoover obliged the Argentineans by sending them Ernest Tutt, an official in the Textile Division of the Bureau of Foreign and Domestic Commerce, who was paid $6,000 a year to survey land and advise Argentineans on increasing their production.

As the fledgling school's students spread out across the world, the chief threat to the United States' expansion was trade policy — its partners' and its own. Keynes, in his famous passage, was not celebrating the stability of international trade. He was mordantly warning how deeply the war had damaged his Londoner's easy access to the goods of the world. "While the citizens of the former warring nations are individually resuming trade relations," wrote another contemporary observer, "governmental policy and politics are still dominated by war psychology" — namely, nationalism, which in policy means protection.

Before the war, tariffs and other barriers to free trade had been falling. In Europe, low duties and reciprocal trade agree-

ments were in favor. Even the United States, which had historically depended on tariffs for revenue as much as for protection, had dropped its tariff rates (a move helped by passage of the federal income tax in 1913). The war had reversed these trends. In Europe, the exhausted powers declared that they were no longer bound by their prewar treaties and raised tariffs to resurrect their war-starved native industries. Meanwhile, American voters turned out the Democrats and returned pro-tariff Republicans to power.

With tariffs uniformly high, the debate over trade diplomacy focused on the concept of reciprocity — the practice of lowering duties on imports coming from certain trading partners, or "most-favored nations," in return for the same preferential treatment. Reciprocity provided a way to keep tariff regimes in place while making it clear that your ports were open for business. It was the economic flip side of the "open-door" policy that the world powers had enforced on China trade in the early years of the century.

The key advocate for reciprocity was a visionary School of Foreign Service professor (and Hoover Commerce Department employee) named William Smith Culbertson. Raised in Pennsylvania, Culbertson had distinguished himself as a law student at Yale University with a book-length essay on the ideas and career of Alexander Hamilton (the last chapter of which is "Protection") that won its author the prestigious John A. Porter Prize. After earning a Ph.D. from Yale, he joined the District of Columbia bar in 1915 and the next year joined the Federal Trade Commission as a special counsel. Two years later he became president of the U.S. Tariff Commission.

A mild-looking man with a high forehead and soft features, Culbertson was a prodigious speaker and a practically nonstop writer who didn't shy away from big topics (or daunting titles) in a 40-year publishing career: *Commercial Policy in War Time and After*; *International Economic Policies: A Survey of the Eco-*

FIELD WORK
In 1920, a group of early SFS students toured South America to investigate political and trade conditions in South American countries under the auspices of the International High Commission, a panel that grew out of the Pan American Financial Conference. The trip was led by Guillermo Sherwell, front right, next to Father Walsh and Constantine McGuire. At center, in white, is director general of the Pan American Union, Leo S. Rowe.

1919
FOREIGN SERVICE CLASS
GEORGETOWN UNIVERSITY

UNDER WAY
The opening lecture for the
School of Foreign Service
on October 2, 1919.

nomics of Diplomacy, Liberation, the Threat and Challenge of Power; and, inevitably, *Reciprocity: A Natural Policy for Foreign Trade*. Remembered as a diplomat as much as a trade official, Culbertson served as ambassador to Romania and Chile for much of the late 1920s and early '30s.

As head of the U.S. Tariff Commission from 1922 to 1925, Culbertson championed reciprocity as the only way for the United States to continue to expand its trade at a time when its competitors and partners were clamping down. He also saw trade diplomacy as the antidote to the nationalism that threatened to lead the world back into war. Not least, foreign trade would put dollars in the hands of the allies and former enemies that owed the United States millions in war reparations and loans, giving them the best chance of payment.

Early on, Culbertson lost these battles. With Republicans returned to power in the 1920 election, protectionism gained momentum as the booming trade of the war years lost steam. He supported the harshly protectionist Fordney-McCumber Act in 1922 because its tariffs at least punished all countries uniformly — a prerequisite for the reciprocity idea that all comers started with the same deal. But it wasn't until the middle of the Great Depression, after the disaster of the Smoot-Hawley Act, that Congress would fall in line with Culbertson's ideas.

Long before then, however, Culbertson's contemplation of how reciprocity could be achieved led him to a more far-reaching vision. As early as 1920, in a speech to the National Foreign Trade Convention, Culbertson dismissed as impractical the idea of negotiating reciprocal treaties with 30 or more countries. "It is doubtful whether American foreign commerce can be greatly advanced in the long run by the negotiation of a series of reciprocity treaties," he said. "The task would be colossal."

Instead, Culbertson argued, the world community needed an international trade arbiter, a standing body that would set tariffs to guarantee fairness for all countries and then meet regularly to adjust rates and police violators. By the time this notion became a reality in 1947, Culbertson had gone on to other things, but those he encountered at Georgetown would help see through his idea of a multilateral trade treaty and a global organization to enforce it.

One of those who acted on Culbertson's ideas was Anthony Kenkel, a graduate assistant in Professor William Notz's third-year Economics course who later worked for Culbertson at the U.S. Tariff Commission.

Kenkel is in many respects representative of those who attended the school during its first years. Kenkel grew up in St. Louis, the son of Swiss immigrants who spoke German at home, according to his son, the retired University of Ottawa

"As head of the U.S. Tariff Commission from 1922 to 1925, Culbertson championed reciprocity as the only way for the United States to continue to expand its trade at a time when its competitors and partners were clamping down."

economic historian James Kenkel. A nanny added French. (His early exposure to foreign languages and other nationalities was typical of the experience of many students from Kenkel's time. He would also "acquire" Italian, says James Kenkel, and pick up Russian at school. He was proficient enough in Latin to return to Georgetown to teach it in later years.)

When the United States joined the war in Europe, Kenkel enlisted in the Marines but before the conflict was over returned to St. Louis for a short stay in the hospital before moving to Washington. There he worked at the Fuel Commission, a wartime agency tasked with managing emergency limits on coal consumption. The commission was disbanded in May of 1919, but the use of commodities had clearly caught Kenkel's interest. He enrolled in the School of Foreign Service that fall. That same year, Culbertson had begun teaching two classes — Political Science, an elective for first-year students, and Commercial Policies and Treaties for third-year students.

Notz, who would become the SFS dean, had come to Georgetown from the Tariff Commission, where he had headed the Export Trade Division, suggesting that Kenkel had gotten his start there through his economics professor. James Kenkel recalls, however, that it was Culbertson who secured his father his job, and the subject of Anthony Kenkel's 1924 master's thesis, "Germany's Raw Material and Foodstuff Problems Prior to 1914," is a clue that Culbertson, for whom equal access to raw materials was a central topic, had some effect on Kenkel.

As an economist at the commission, Kenkel's primary responsibility came to be sugar. Americans never grew as much sugar as they consumed, making imports a necessity greeted warily by domestic sugar farmers, who demanded stiff tariffs to protect — but most of all to stabilize — their prices. As a result, sugar was one of the biggest revenue producers under the customs law. Complicat-

NAFTA

Forging the Global Economy

IN 1991, THE NORTH AMERICAN FREE TRADE Agreement negotiations began as an initiative by the George H.W. Bush administration's State Department. At that time, Andrew Shoyer, who had earned a combined J.D./M.S.F.S. in 1986, was a 31-year-old lawyer in the office of the general counsel of the United States Trade Representative. He tells the story of how he ended up writing the first sections of what would become the most-discussed trade deal in recent memory.

"One day Julius Katz, the deputy United States Trade Representative, came to my office and asked me to draft some chapters for a trade agreement with Mexico. If I was being asked to do it, believe me, it was not important to the agency. At the time, the USTR office was focused on the Uruguay Round [of the GATT negotiations], which would ultimately result in the founding of the World Trade Organization. Our boss, U.S. Trade Representative Carla Hills, thought making a deal with Mexico would be a distraction. But she tasked Katz to start the main thinking, and since my client desks were North America and Latin America, he asked me.

"We had just concluded a free-trade agreement with Canada a few years before, so I didn't have to invent anything. The basic architecture was there. I started with basic rules on trade

TRADE BOOSTER *President William J. Clinton (SFS'68) participating in a NAFTA Products Event on the South Lawn of the White House in 1993.*

and goods, sections on agriculture, energy, autos, then moved to government procurement, services, and investment. When I took Katz the six chapters, he was shocked to see me. I still remember the look on his face. I think he had forgotten that he had asked me.

"That was sort of the beginning. We continued taking pieces of the Canada Free Trade Agreement and expanding them into something that looked like it might work for Mexico. When it became a trilateral negotiation they got a real lawyer, Ken Freiberg, to be the lead lawyer, and I became the deputy legal advisor. It quickly took over my life, which was a delight for anyone who lives for something like this.

"What was particularly fascinating was watching the Mexican negotiators. They were brilliant, largely U.S.-educated — they all had Ph.D.s from Stanford — and they were using us as leverage to modernize the Mexican economic system. They needed the United States negotiators to insist that certain things be in the agreement so they could say, 'It's not me — the gringos are asking for this. We have to do it.' We so admired them because we recognized what they were trying to accomplish.

"That's not to say the negotiation wasn't difficult. We had our own issues. We were still coming out of the oil shocks of the late 1970s,

and we were really concerned to prohibit these two energy behemoths on either side of us from restricting exports of energy to us [as the Middle Eastern countries had done]. This became chapter six of the NAFTA. We incorporated provisions that said you can't restrict exports or put restrictions on export taxes.

"We negotiated in Dallas, in Ottawa and Toronto, in Mexico City a couple of times. Someone had a concert T-shirt made with all the stops on the back, which I still have. The big push at the end was at the Watergate Hotel here in Washington. We took over lots of rooms and, depending on the topic, different agencies took the lead in each room. In the financial-services room, the Treasury Department tended to have the lead. With energy and agriculture, it was the Commerce Department. I would go from room to room trying to listen, doing whatever I could to help.

"The way you negotiate is you get the whole deal on paper and show where you disagree by putting the disputed language in square brackets. Then you work through all the alternatives. We had all these typographical devices to show what each of the three countries wanted. This was before the internet, so we were working with floppy disks on laptops. If we were negotiating late at night, which we often were, you had to fight about who had control of the keyboard.

"One night I realized a long, tedious list had been deleted. I had to retype the whole thing. So it's not false humility to say that, while I didn't really write the NAFTA, I did type the NAFTA."

ing the sugar question further was the fact that Cuba, one of the world's biggest growers of sugar cane — most of it owned by American firms — depended entirely on the U.S. sugar trade. Two recent tariff rate hikes, in 1922 and 1930, had sent Cuba's economy reeling.

Kenkel was put to work on a permanent fix to this delicate problem after Congress, under pressure to boost trade as the economy continued to drag through the middle-1930s, passed the liberalizing Reciprocal Trade Act of 1934, which gave the president the power, for the first time in history, to make tariff deals without going through the Senate for approval. Kenkel, who had been meeting with the Cubans since 1927, now made a deal that reduced tariffs on sugar exports from $2 per pound to under a penny. In return, Cuba would take more American goods. From 1933 to 1935, exports to Cuba increased 140 percent.

The Reciprocal Trade Act is considered the key to convincing not just the U.S. Congress but the world that low tariffs promote global commerce that is both profitable and peaceful. In that sense, Kenkel's deal with Cuba led directly to his work on the General Agreement on Tariffs and Trade after the Second World War, which laid the foundation for the World Trade Organization and the architecture of global trade that we know today. Kenkel was one of eight U.S. Tariff Commission representatives who attended the first talks in Geneva, and he was a delegate to the 1950 and 1951 rounds as well. He continued as the commission's top adviser on GATT issues in 1964.

By then, Kenkel had spent the final 15 years of his career on GATT issues. He died in Bladensburg, Maryland, in 1986 at the age of 92.

While the School of Foreign Service was stocking the government with able trade officials, it was also training practitioners. The number who entered business straight out of Georgetown was hindered, first by the Depression and then by the Second World War, but as the veterans came home and trade picked up in the wake of the war, SFS alumni forged new businesses based on the international view of commerce that they'd received at school.

An example of these entrepreneurial-minded graduates is William Howard McCandless, Jr., an Eagle Scout from Sterling, Illinois, who traveled abroad in 1933, at the age of 17, to attend an International Boy Scout Jamboree in Hungary. The experience seems to have sparked a sense of adventure in McCandless. While at Antioch College in Ohio, he worked off-campus at a Sears store and was excited to learn that the company was busy expanding overseas. If he was going to make a business career, McCandless wrote in a self-published memoir before his death in 2006, "I began to realize that I needed courses such as Spanish and Political Science and Law, which Antioch did not offer." In September 1936, he transferred to the School of Foreign Service.

After graduation in 1939, he headed to New York to take a job translating the Montgomery Ward catalog into Spanish; he'd not only studied the language for three years at Georgetown, he'd also spent his last college summer in Mexico City studying at a university. Once McCandless got to New York, however, an acquaintance arranged for the SFS grad to meet Nelson Rockefeller, then the 31-year-old vice president of the Chase Manhattan Bank. Rockefeller got him a job working for U.S. Steel as an

EXPORT EXPERTISE
William Howard
McCandless Jr. from
Domesday Booke 1939.

"Everhard (SFS'58) was also an important voice in the import-export industry at a time when the business's infrastructure and regulatory framework were rapidly changing."

TARIFF KILLER
President Franklin Roosevelt signs the Reciprocal Trade Agreements Act into law in 1934.

export clerk in the corporation's New York office.

That job was short-lived, as steel orders dried up in a Europe plummeting into war. McCandless had learned enough about exporting to land a similar job with a maker of industrial leather belts in Worcester, Massachusetts, but soon McCandless found himself at war. "When he volunteered, he hoped to get into translation," recalls his wife, Eleanor McCandless. Instead the Navy sent him to New Orleans, from where, as one of four officers on a submarine chaser, he left for the Pacific via the Panama Canal.

After his discharge from the Navy he returned, now married, to New Orleans, Mrs. McCandless's hometown. With his relatively thin experience — and a loan of $1,500 from a local bank — he founded his own freight-forwarding firm, expediting cargo coming down the Mississippi River to its destinations overseas. "If someone in Chicago wants to ship something to South America, they had to have someone at the port to handle the paperwork and deal with customs," explains McCandless's son, William McCandless III. "They had to have them booked on a ship at the port of export." McCandless named his venture McCandless & Company, though when he began in September of 1945, the company consisted of him working from a desk that he shared for $17 a month.

He built the business based on a straightforward idea: "At the time, manufacturers located in the Middle West were sending their export shipments through New York, then the only known 'gateway to the world'," McCandless wrote in his memoir. "But why not send them through New Orleans? It took no longer, and I discovered and proved it was no more expensive." His first client was a maker of saw mills, who sent a used model via McCandless & Co. to the Philippines. Traversing the middle of the country in his old Ford and making business calls in his Navy uniform — the only good set of clothes he could afford at the time — McCandless slowly built a roster of clients. "I earned the reputation of being

SHIPPING TERMINAL
Piers in Hoboken, New Jersey, late in New York Harbor's heyday as a hub for foreign export and import. Container ships would soon shift the shipping business down the coast to Elizabeth and other updated ports.

> "The Navy sent [McCandless] to New Orleans, from where, as one of four officers on a submarine chaser, he left for the Pacific via the Panama Canal."

the first international freight forwarder to visit the city of Denver."

The cornerstone of his success was an account with Phillips Petroleum, which retained him in 1947. By 1960, his client list included Samsonite, Hallmark Cards and other internationally known brands.

McCandless's prosperity was not solely his own doing, of course. In the decades before World War II, the Port of New Orleans had expanded aggressively, with a dozen new wharves and the construction of the Inner Harbor Navigation Canal linking the Mississippi with Lake Pontchartrain. In the 1950s, a new rail terminal was built. But McCandless took full advantage of New Orleans's rebirth as a port. Besides drawing new shippers to the city, he was instrumental in expanding its reach beyond routes to South America, in which New Orleans had a clear geographic advantage over New York, to China and Africa.

But the ultimate foundation for his success was his impetuous desire to do business and communicate with other nations. "He would go down to the docks to see where the shipments were from," often speaking Spanish with seamen from the boats to gain insights into the direction his business needed to go, remembers Eleanor McCandless.

Bill McCandless was hardly the last to make a career of the maritime education he got at Georgetown. Rolf Williams, who had

Carroll Quigley

CARROLL QUIGLEY WAS BORN IN BOSTON AND attended Harvard University, where he received bachelor's, master's, and doctoral degrees. He taught at Princeton and Harvard before continuing his teaching career at Georgetown University, where he taught in the School of Foreign Service from 1941 to 1976. However, throughout his 35-year tenure on campus, Quigley did not limit himself to university work: During the '50s, he acted as a consultant for the Defense Department, the House Select Committee on Aeronautics and Space Exploration, and the Navy. In addition, he advised the Smithsonian on the American history department of what would become the National Museum of American History. Despite these many projects, Quigley's principal occupation and passion remained teaching. While at Georgetown, he taught a foundational course entitled Development of Civilizations, which many SFS alumni cite as the most impactful course of their undergraduate careers. President Bill Clinton (SFS'68) named Quigley as a major influence during his presidential campaign, even referencing him in his 1992 Democratic National Convention speech. In Clinton's autobiography, *My Life*, he calls Development of Civilizations "the most legendary class at Georgetown." Quigley was proud of the impact he was able to have on students; during the war, he even volunteered to teach college algebra when he learned that

SFS graduates were struggling to gain officer positions because they lacked sufficient math backgrounds. As his colleagues were called up to serve in the war, Quigley took on their classes. He couldn't understand why he hadn't been drafted but soon learned the answer when Father Walsh, the school's founder, told him: "You were left here because I insisted on it." Throughout his career, Quigley emphasized "inclusive

diversity," the ability of Western civilization to adapt and absorb new ideas, which he identified as the West's greatest strength. Quigley was the author of two books, *Evolution of Civilization* and *Tragedy and Hope: The World in Our Time*, as well as many academic papers. Quigley retired in June 1976 after receiving the Faculty Award from students for the fourth consecutive year. He passed away in January 1977.

A PASSION FOR TEACHING
Quigley's courses have been cited by President Bill Clinton, and other students, as the most impactful in their undergraduate careers.

Walter Giles

WALTER GILES, BORN IN OKLAHOMA, WAS A lifelong Hoya. Having graduated from the SFS in 1943, then serving in Air Force Intelligence for the rest of the war, he returned to Georgetown to obtain both a master's and a Ph.D., which he completed in 1956 before becoming a professor. Giles taught various classes in the field of government but quickly gained notoriety for his U.S. Constitution and Government class, his rigorous teaching style, and his biting wit. A stickler for rules, Giles reportedly would lock the doors to the lecture hall five minutes past the start of class to shut out late arrivals. Students unprepared for the lecture ahead had the option of approaching their professor at the start of class and stating "Nolo contendere"—literally, "I do not want to compete"—in order to avoid the embarrassment of being cold-called and having no answer. In his memoir, *My Life*, Bill Clinton cites Giles as one of his greatest influences. In one memorable incident, Giles noticed Clinton napping in the first row. Giles continued his lecture, loudly declaiming that one Supreme Court ruling was so clear that it was impossible to misunderstand—"unless, of course, you're from some hick town in Arkansas." Clinton, a native of Hope, Arkansas, jolted awake to the sound of laughter bouncing off the walls of the lecture hall. Clinton never fell asleep in one of Giles's classes again. Despite the difficulty of Giles's classes, alumni who took them recognized this was only a

LIFELONG HOYA
Giles, a stickler for the rules and a friend to students, played a prominent role in fighting for SFS's independent identity.

result of the professor's high expectations, which ultimately pushed them to appreciate his style and personality. Giles would even invite students back to his home to watch football, enjoy a beer, and eat crackers topped with cheese and bacon. His friendliness with students made its way into the classroom, too: Each spring he would hold his famous Madison Martini Lecture, in which he explained the system of checks and balances woven into the Constitution by James Madison. As he spoke he would make martinis, a drink that he considered an apt metaphor for the balance between the three branches of government. Each ingredient (gin, vermouth, and olive) was in perfect proportion. If one became too strong, it would overpower the others, and the whole drink would be spoiled.

In addition to his popularity among students and the renown of his class, Giles ought to be remembered as a savior of the School of Foreign Service itself. To some extent, Giles deserves credit for preventing the SFS from sliding into irrelevance. Following the retirement in 1952 and then death in 1956 of the school's founder, Father Edmund A. Walsh, S.J., the SFS's autonomy within Georgetown was gradually chipped away: It lost control over its budget, curriculum, and admissions. Between 1955 and 1970, the school did not even have its own distinct faculty, which Father Walsh previously had handpicked for their skill as instructors. These developments prompted the Middle States Association of Colleges and Secondary Schools to question whether "anything remained of the School of Foreign Service except its name." In an April 1968 issue of *The Hoya*, Giles criticized the school's lack of independent faculty and departments under the headline "SFS Losing Identity." Amid student protests led by the "Save our School Committee," Giles, along with Professor Carroll Quigley, continuously pushed for the creation of an SFS core faculty, which was eventually granted by Georgetown president Father Robert J. Henle, S.J. Giles passed away in October 2009.

come to Georgetown from a shipping-services family in Norfolk, Virginia, in the late 1930s, returned to his father's ship chandlery, Anders Williams & Co., after serving in the U.S. Navy during World War II. According to family lore, Williams told his father his employment was temporary. He stayed for 50 years, during which time he founded a ship agency that became the largest in Hampton Roads, a marine lubicrant-supply company, and a trucking company to move freight to and from the port. Williams passed away in 2005, leaving his son, also named Rolf, as owner of Anders Williams.

Perhaps the most colorful, and notable, foreign-service graduate in the shipping business was Conrad H.C. Everhard. Born in the Netherlands in 1931, Everhard came to the United States to attend Georgetown and took a job with the United States Lines after graduating in 1958. By the early 1970s, Everhard was CEO of Dart Container Line, a consortium of European shipping companies headquartered in New York that was among the first to use containers.

A spirited debater and sought-after public speaker, he was known in the New York and New Jersey ports — and at Manhattan's old-school Whitehall Club — for his candor and humor in meetings and with the shipping press. He was part of "a now-extinct 'Mad Men generation' of post-World War II shipping executives who cut deals over lunchtime martinis," according to his son, Conrad E. Everhard, who graduated from SFS in 1981. As CEO of the Orient Overseas Container Line, which had bought out Dart, the elder Everhard described his relations with headquarters in Hong Kong as perfectly satisfactory. "We have a relationship of trust and understanding," he said. "They don't trust me, and I can't understand them."

Though he cut a flamboyant figure, Everhard was also an important voice in the import-export industry at a time when the business's infrastructure and regulatory framework were

> **"If Everhard represented a dying breed of shipping executives, he was also the last to represent the School of Foreign Service's early focus on the nuts and bolts of oceangoing trade."**

rapidly changing. Having helmed Dart, a small but pioneering company, through the container revolution in shipping, Everhard fought efforts by the Reagan administration to introduce more competition into an industry in which, in the name of efficiency, rates traditionally were set and goods assigned to ships by the collective will of the shipping lines in "conference."

In 1990, President George H.W. Bush appointed him to a Presidential Advisory Commission on Conferences in Ocean Shipping, which was charged with recommending legislative updates to the Shipping Act of 1984. Everhard argued, along with other shipping executives, that unleashed competition would bring the same rate wars and mergers that had stressed the airline companies.

He lost the argument. With the Ocean Shipping Reform Act of 1998, the conference system, while not outlawed, was severely limited. Everhard continued to offer ideas that were as engaging as they were contrarian. In 2000, he spoke at the Port Industry Day in New York, where officials had released plans for massively expanded facilities, raising doubts about the relentless growth of oceangoing vessels. Larger ships require expensive dredging that favors bigger ports over regional ones, concentrating highway congestion and disrupting the underwater environment.

If Everhard represented a dying breed of shipping execu-

REVOLUTION AT SEA
Opposite, moving freight on a wharf for Orient Overseas Container Line.

WAR FOOTING
Father Walsh
walking with General
Douglas MacArthur
in Tokyo, 1948.

tives, he was also the last to represent the School of Foreign Service's early focus on the nuts and bolts of oceangoing trade. By the time he passed away in 2014, the concerns of the school, and of those who went into fields associated with overseas trade, had been transformed.

Some of the change had to do with the work of government economists such as Anthony Kenkel and fellow SFS alum Alfred Powers, who had helped GATT set tariffs at uniformly low rates in the decades following World War II. As tariff protection was taken off the table, countries began protecting their home markets through trade-inhibiting regulations and other obstacles. While in the 1980s and early 1990s the United States went through a spasm of protectionism spurred by the rise of Japan's car industry and the collapse of American steel, Western countries increasingly put their faith in the multilateral, free-trade regime presaged by GATT and ultimately enshrined in the creation of the World Trade Organization in the Uruguay Round in 1994.

But trade had also changed because the U.S. economy had changed. Over the course of the 20th century, the country shifted away from manufactured goods to services — technological know-how, consulting and legal expertise — and to entertainment produced in easily pirated digital form. The shift to trade in ideas

> "In a sense I was swept into foreign service on the wave of a growing involvement in world affairs of the 1920s, which washed our country from the fundament of isolation in which it seemed to be resting securely."
>
> — CHARLES BALDWIN (SFS'26)

in turn led the conversation away from barriers at a trading partner's border to questions of copyrights and intellectual property.

That change has made for a different kind of trade professional. Born in Richmond, Virginia, Victoria Espinel grew up in Washington, DC, but often visited her father's family in his native Colombia, where, she says, she became conscious of political unrest and the threat of rebel violence. She had decided early in life that she would attend Georgetown — her mother, Jeanne Lord, was Associate Vice President for Student Affairs at the university — but her personal experience in South America convinced her to attend the School of Foreign Service.

Between receiving her B.S.F.S. in 1989 and her J.D. from Georgetown Law, Espinel interned at the Commerce Department's National Telecommunications and Information Administration. The goal of learning international telecommunications law prompted her to move to the United Kingdom and attend the London School of Economics in the mid-1990s. On arriving at the school, however, she found that a key telecommuications expert was on sabbatical.

Espinel instead delved into copyright law, focusing on its applications to the still-embryonic internet, which led to a job with the Washington, DC, law firm Covington & Burling in London. "I worked all over eastern Europe as these countries were coming out of Communism," Espinel says.

Her experience drew the attention of the U.S. Trade Representative's office in Washington, where she returned in 2001 to establish its Office of Intellectual Property and Innovation, serving as the first chief trade negotiator for intellectual property. Working on 18 different trade agreements, she created the template for how American patents would be translated into protections overseas. Soon she was advising the White House on enforcement of copyrights domestically and abroad, and in

"Map of the Modern World" Creator: Charles Pirtle

MAP OF THE MODERN WORLD IS ONE OF THOSE mandatory classes at the School of Foreign Service that current students look upon with a mix of emotions. In the age of Google, it may strike one as redundant to learn every country's capital in addition to the world's major waterways, mountain ranges, and tectonic boundaries. Nevertheless, the class has come to be seen as a rite of passage. Once they have completed it, students recognize that Map, as it is colloquially known, is about far more than rote memorization. It provides the basis of knowledge that any budding foreign-service officer, international businessperson, or non-profit worker requires to tackle global issues and understand the geographic forces that have molded the world we live in. The characteristics and shape of the land, the seas, and the rivers are fundamental to the business of international relations: Industry, trade, interstate relations, and culture are all affected by geographic features. Although today the term "geographic determinism" is considered in some academic circles to be somewhat pejorative, the rising spectres of resource scarcity, water politics, and climate change demand a full comprehension of the Map of the Modern World. For this class, we have Professor Charles Pirtle to thank. Pirtle began teaching at the School of Foreign Service in 1982, and also served as an Associate Dean, Director of the BSFS Program, Dean of Faculty,

and Director of the Fellows Program. Map was his creation. Before coming to Georgetown, Pirtle served in the U.S. Air Force following graduation from high school. After his military service, he enrolled in Kent State University in Ohio, earning both bachelor's and master's degrees. His course work was focused in the sciences; he wrote his master's thesis on forest hydrology. Following Kent State, he matriculated at the University of Pittsburgh with a Ph.D. in geography, though he switched midway through to a focus on international relations. During his tenure at Georgetown, Pirtle was known as a "geopolitical legend." This is reflected in the fondness alumni show for him. Parag Khanna (SFS'99, SSP'05), former senior geopolitical advisor at the U.S. Special Operations in Iraq and Afghanistan and foreign-policy advisor to

Barack Obama's first presidential campaign, wrote a book in 2016 entitled *Connectography: Mapping the Future of Global Civilization.* Khanna called Map "the legendary course at SFS," and said that "everything [Khanna has] written since 1999 has been grappling with the lessons of Charles Pirtle's classes." Indeed, at the University of Pennsylvania, a student wrote an op-ed in which she expressed her desire for her college to offer a course modeled after Map of the Modern World. How, she asks her readers, are UPenn graduates supposed to become future leaders of the world if they don't know the information taught in Map? For the article, she interviewed a Georgetown student who said that she can "see any news story from around the globe and immediately place that story in a geographic context."

GEOPOLITICAL LEGEND
Professor Pirtle, the creator of the legendary class Map of the Modern World, which has been a staple of alumni nostalgia ever since.

Jan Karski

JAN KARSKI WAS BORN IN ŁÓDŹ, POLAND, IN
1914. He began his career as both a soldier
and a diplomat for the Second Polish Republic
that existed between the world wars. However,
in September 1939, Poland was invaded by
both the Soviet Union and Nazi Germany, after
which Karski joined the Polish underground
resistance, known as the Home Army. During
one mission he was captured and tortured by
Nazis but managed to escape to continue his
mission: to smuggle information in and out of
Poland from the Polish underground forces
to the government-in-exile and Allied powers.
Karski is best known for his efforts to uncover
the Holocaust. Twice, Karski broke into the
Warsaw ghetto to report on the egregious
conditions there, and he once disguised himself
as a camp guard at a transit station for Jews
on their way to the Bełżec death camp. In the
course of his mission to let the world know
about Nazi atrocities, Karski relayed what he
had witnessed to prominent Allied leaders,
but his pleas largely led to inaction. In an Oval
Office meeting with President Roosevelt, Karski
was stunned when Roosevelt's response to
his story made no mention of the plight of the
Jewish people. In 1944, Karski wrote *Story of
a Secret State*, his World War II memoir and
one of the first accounts of the Holocaust. The
book quickly became a bestseller and led to his
doing a speaking tour in the U.S. and Canada.

**DIPLOMATIC
RESISTANCE FIGHTER**
*First to report to Allied
Powers about Nazi
plans to exterminate
the Jewish people.*

It was republished in 2014 by Georgetown
University Press with a foreword by Madeleine
Albright. Following the war, Karski settled in
Washington and obtained a doctorate from
Georgetown, after which he began a 40-year
teaching career on the Hilltop. Karski was
popular among students and faculty alike. Frank
Murray (SFS'72) recalls witnessing Karski walk
through a cloud of tear gas during the May
1972 antiwar protests occuring on campus. In
full view of students, tears streamed down his
face from his reddened eyes. When asked why
he did it, the professor replied, "I had never
experienced tear gas." Professor John Bailey, a
colleague of Karski's, described him as "a very

effective teacher, extraordinarily smart and
sharp. [And] he was someone who cared about
his students." In 1982, Karski was awarded
the title of "Righteous Among the Nations,"
an award to honor non-Jews who risked
their lives to save Jews from the Holocaust,
by Yad Vashem, Israel's memorial for the
Holocaust. Twelve years later, Israel declared
him an honorary citizen. Following the fall of
Communism, Poland granted him two awards:
the Order of the White Eagle and the Virtuti
Militari, the highest civilian and military honors,
respectively. Posthumously, Karski received the
Presidential Medal of Freedom from President
Obama. Jan Karski passed away in 2000.

2009, President Obama named her the nation's first "IP czar."

At the White House, Espinel focused on digital piracy, cracking down on the illegal downloading of movies and music by enlisting the aid of search engines and credit-card companies as well as the entertainment industry. Although not officially involved, Espinel helped with a 2012 agreement, known as the "six strikes" program, between the movie and recording industries and internet service providers to threaten the accounts of serial illegal downloaders.

Defending Hollywood and the work of U.S. "content creators" from piratical downloads abroad is a long way from arranging sugar tariff rates. Where once farmers and other major exporters watched trade battles closely, the interconnectedness of the world has broadened Americans' interests. "Over time, women's groups, churches, NGOs, labor groups have all gotten involved," says Wendy Silberman Cutler (MSFS'83), whose three decades as a negotiator at the USTR was capped by her tenure as Acting Deputy U.S. Trade Negotiator and a lead role in the Trans-Pacific Partnership. "The AARP became active in TPP because they were concerned about access to pharmaceuticals," she says. "When I first started in trade, you'd never have that."

The complexity of trade agreements has grown with the number of stakeholders, as has the expertise required on the part of trade specialists. Cutler, who got a Master of Science in Foreign Service from SFS in 1983, has helped negotiate agreements on financial services, insurance, telecommunications and semiconductors. As trade becomes a primary thrust of U.S. diplomacy, trade agreements have become the focus of advocacy on topics not traditionally associated with trade at all: environmental concerns, treatment of workers and the loss of manufacturing.

If the early trade-oriented classes at the School of Foreign Service would not recognize the expansive scope of trade deals today, students like Halleck Butts, who shipped out for

the Far East in 1920 before he'd even graduated, would likely recognize the United States' continuing "pivot" to Asia. Cutler's work with the TPP was an extension of the work she did as chief negotiator on the U.S.-Korea (KORUS) free-trade agreement signed in 2007. She spent most of her 32 years in government engaging with countries of the Pacific Rim, primarily Japan, occasionally dealing with a 1986 SFS graduate, Taro Kono, a onetime trade negotiator and now foreign minister. Cutler is now managing director of the Washington, DC, office of the Asia Society Policy Institute.

If Cutler and Espinel demonstrate the persistent connection between the School of Foreign Service and the Commerce Department, generations of post-World War II graduates reveal another arc of the school's history, this one away from trade and toward a new emphasis on diplomacy.

This movement is captured in the distinguished career of Charles Baldwin, President John F. Kennedy's ambassador to Malaya, who received his degree from SFS in 1926. Hired by the Commerce Department's automotive division the next year, Baldwin was sent to Australia, where he spent two happy years as a U.S. trade commissioner, according to his son, C. Stephen Baldwin. On his return to Washington, he worked out of the department's mammoth new building on Constitution Avenue. He married and built a home in what was then a very rural Bethesda, Maryland. But after the Pearl Harbor attacks, Baldwin joined the U.S. Navy and was assigned to London as an intelligence officer; at the war's conclusion in 1945, he reentered civilian service as an employee of the State Department.

As a foreign-service officer, Baldwin was still primarily tasked with economic relations, as he had been at Commerce, and he eventually became Assistant Secretary of State for Far Eastern Economic Affairs. But as he completed tours in Santi-

ago, London (again), Singapore and Oslo, Baldwin was increasingly pulled into political diplomacy. As the fate of the city of Trieste was being settled in the postwar scramble in Europe, Baldwin, then an economic counselor in Norway, was sent as one of the first Foreign Policy Advisors, or POLADs, to assist Major General Earl Hoag and his British counterpart, General Terrence Aire, with the diplomatic aspects of the tug-of-war between Yugoslavia and Italy over Trieste.

In 1961, Baldwin was drafted by JFK to represent the United States in the Federation of Malaya, which then comprised what are today Singapore and Malaysia. At the time, the country was facing a communist insurgency, and Baldwin, attuned to Washington's fixation on the domino theory and the brewing conflict in Vietnam, represented the advantages of democracy, his son says, with "an uncompromising American-ness."

Baldwin's transition from commercial diplomat to ambassador in a critical zone of U.S. influence is emblematic of the shifting concerns of the country, and of the School of Foreign Service. He was quite conscious of his own shift "away from provincialism" toward a global worldview, an evolution that began in 1925 when he took a break from his studies at Georgetown to sail on the *SS Steel Mariner*, a merchant ship owned by U.S. Steel. Chipping rust from the ship's deck plates in the middle of the South Pacific, Baldwin later wrote, was the first step toward his career in the foreign service. "In a sense I was swept into foreign service on the wave of a growing involvement in world affairs of the 1920s, which washed our country from the fundament of isolation in which it seemed to be resting securely," he recalls in his 1984 memoir, *An Ambassador's Journey*.

That same rising wave was about to lift the School of Foreign Service out of its origins as a merchant-marine trade school into a bulwark of the American Century.

TECH DRIVEN
The trade deals negotiated by Victoria Espinel, opposite, concern types of goods the earliest SFS students never learned about, delivered over virtual routes that they would have had a hard time imagining.

Heads of State

1. Zeljko Komsic, Tripartite President of Bosnia, 2006–present, SFS'82; **2. Bill Clinton,** President of the United States, 1993–2001, SFS'68; **3. Ricardo Arias,** President of Panama, 1955–56, SFS'35; **4. Gloria Macapagal-Arroyo,** President of the Philippines, 2001–10, attended SFS 1964–66;
5. Galo Plaza President of Ecuador, 1948–52, SFS'29;
6. His Majesty King Abdullah II bin al-Hussein, King of Jordan, 1999–present, MSFS Mid-Career Fellow '87; **7. Dalia Grybauskaitė,** President of Lithuania, 2009–19, Pew Economic Freedom Fellow '92; **8. His Majesty King Felipe VI,** King of Spain, 2014–present, MSFS'95

100 Years of Leadership: SFS Deans

Roy S. MacElwee, Ph.D.
1921–1923

Roy S. MacElwee became the first Dean of the School of Foreign Service in 1921. Previously serving as the Director of the Bureau of Foreign and Domestic Commerce of the U.S. Commerce Department, MacElwee helped to shape the School's early focus on teaching applicable skills in commerce and trade. "If America had had a West Point or an Annapolis of shipping in operation for years before the war we would have been ready to meet the shipping emergencies of the situation with far greater skill than we did and at incalculable money-saving to the country," The *Washington Post* quoted him as saying in September 1921.

William F. Notz, Ph.D.
1925–1935

William F. Notz was a prominent economist and Chief of the Export Trade Division of the Federal Trade Commission. Throughout its history, the SFS has adapted its curriculum to address the pressing problems of the current era; Notz's tenure was no exception. Leading the SFS during the beginning of the Great Depression, Notz helped oversee the curriculum's shift toward domestic business and economics in the direction of national reconstruction.

Thomas H. Healy, Ph.D.
1935–1943

Upon the attack on Pearl Harbor and the U.S.'s entry into World War II, Thomas H. Healy reorganized the SFS curriculum and introduced an accelerated program of study in order to meet the needs of wartime. Vacations were shortened and summer sessions were added so that students could complete their degrees in three years before being called up for the draft. Special military-training programs were offered, and language courses relevant to the war were opened to non-SFS students. A required course, The Political Economy of Total War, was also added.

Still, Healy and Father Walsh, then still the regent, were determined to remain true to the School's mission during wartime and to help foster connections among students, faculty, and administration. One student at the time noted that "it was not unusual for the dean, Thomas Healy, to visit a classroom to make an announcement or simply to sit in to see what was going on."

Frank L. Fadner S.J., Ph.D.
ACTING 1950–1958

From its beginning, the leadership of the SFS was in the hands of its founder and longtime regent, Father Walsh. When Walsh fell ill in the early 1950s, Frank L. Fadner, S.J., took over as regent and acting dean, a position that had been left vacant for several years. Fadner was an expert in Russian history who graduated from the SFS in 1932 and joined the Society of Jesus shortly thereafter. Joining the SFS faculty in 1949, he would go on to teach history there for another three decades.

During Fadner's tenure as dean and regent, the SFS's focus began shifting from practical training toward liberal education. "We don't teach courses in geopolitics or staple commodities in world trade any more," Fadner noted in 1959. "We find it much better to give good stiff courses in government, history, and geography. If you do this well, you don't need the razzle-dazzle."

John F. Parr, Ph.D.
1958–1961

John F. Parr graduated from the SFS in 1939 and obtained his master's degree from Georgetown in 1948. He completed his Ph.D. work at the University of Fribourg in Switzerland, where he taught as a professor of history and literature before returning to the SFS. He also served as assistant director of the International Relations Bureau of the National Catholic Welfare Conference.

As Dean of the SFS in 1958, Parr oversaw the opening of the Walsh Building, a new home for the School of Foreign Service named for its founder. At the building's dedication, the School was also officially renamed the Edmund A. Walsh School of Foreign Service.

Parr was also at the helm of SFS for another important milestone in the School's history: the graduation of some of the first full-time women students. By 1960, 111 of the SFS's 845 students were women.

William E. Moran, Jr, LL.B
1963–1966

William E. Moran, Jr., a lawyer with experience in foreign aid, is most notable for initiating reforms in the SFS undergraduate curriculum. Moran served with the Federal Bureau of Investigation during World War II and entered the Foreign Service in 1945. He served as assistant director of the Marshall Plan effort to Belgium from 1949 to 1952, and then went on to direct the Africa Division of the Foreign Operations Administration. He also was director of security arrangements for the atomic tests in the Pacific for the Atomic Energy Commission.

Moran relaxed the SFS's rigid course requirements, allowing for more electives. He also concentrated major fields, combining two vocational majors of international transportation and foreign trade into one academically focused major, international economic affairs. The language programs were strengthened, and a BSFS/MSFS joint-degree program was introduced.

Joseph S. Sebes, S.J.
1966–1968

Joseph S. Sebes, S.J., was an expert in Chinese history who began teaching at Georgetown in 1958. He entered the Society of Jesus in 1934 and spent subsequent years in China, where he was ordained in 1946. Serving as dean during a time of increased—and controversial—U.S. engagement in Asia, Sebes is most notable for his lasting contributions to the study of Asia at Georgetown, spearheading the development of the graduate program in East Asian history.

Jesse A. Mann, Ph.D.
1968–1970

Jesse A. Mann took over the helm of SFS as interim dean during a tumultuous time in the school's history, a period of disorganization and what was essentially an identity crisis. He convened a committee that met every week for nearly two years to try to resolve some of the School's challenges. The most important development that arose from this committee was the concept of a "core faculty," professors whose primary affiliation would be with the SFS but who would also hold secondary membership in their respective departments.

Peter F. Krogh, Ph.D.
1970–1995

After an extensive search, Peter F. Krogh was chosen to become dean of the SFS at the young age of 32. He was previously associate dean of the Tufts University Fletcher School, a White House Fellow, and Special Assistant to the Secretary of State.

Often recognized as the "second founder" of the SFS, Krogh enacted numerous reforms during his tenure as dean that helped shaped the SFS into the institution it is today. Arriving at a school experiencing a great level of division and mistrust among faculty, Krogh built upon Mann's goal to realize a separate SFS faculty. He revised the curriculum, allowing for more electives and professionally oriented courses, stressing the School's interdisciplinary nature. He established a faculty advising system and worked to bolster opportunities for study abroad. Krogh also sought to take advantage of the SFS's location in DC. He introduced "Dean's Seminars," weekly programs that gave students the chance to hear from well-known practitioners followed by informal receptions. He helped promote internship opportunities in the city and took students on tours of the White House, the State Department, and elsewhere.

Krogh also revived the MSFS program and played a key role in the development of several institutions and centers. He was responsible for developing the Landegger Program in International Business Diplomacy, the Institute for the Study of Diplomacy, the Center for Contemporary Arab Studies, and the predecessor to the BMW Center for German and European Studies. The most evident example of Krogh's legacy is the Edward B. Bunn, S.J., Intercultural Center (ICC), which he spearheaded the construction of in the early 1980s to give the quickly expanding SFS a new home.

Robert Gallucci, Ph.D.
1996–2009

Robert Gallucci was appointed dean in 1996 after 21 years of distinguished service in a variety of government positions focusing on international security. As Ambassador-at-Large and Special Envoy for the U.S. Department of State, he dealt with the threats posed by the proliferation of ballistic missiles and weapons of mass destruction. He was chief U.S. negotiator during the North Korean nuclear crisis of 1994 and served as Assistant Secretary of State for Political-Military Affairs and as Deputy Executive Chairman of the UN Special Commission overseeing the disarmament of Iraq following the first Gulf War.

During his tenure as dean, Gallucci facilitated the creation of the School of Foreign Service in Qatar and helped raise Georgetown's master's program in international affairs to a number-one ranking and the undergraduate program to number four, as reported by *Foreign Policy* magazine. He also oversaw the creation of the Program for Jewish Civilization, an interdisciplinary hub of research and teaching, and the Mortara Center for International Studies, whose mission is to bring together scholars and policymakers.

Carol Lancaster, Ph.D
2009–2013

Carol Lancaster, a lifetime Washington DC resident, graduated from the SFS in 1964 and went on to earn a Ph.D. in 1972 at the London School of Economics and Political Science. She was part of the U.S. Department of State's policy-planning staff from 1977 to 1980 and served as Deputy Assistant Secretary of State for Africa from 1980 to 1981. In 1981, she began at the SFS as a research professor and later became director of the African Studies Program. From 1993 to 1996, she was Deputy Administrator of USAID, the first woman to hold this position.

Lancaster was selected as the first woman to serve as the SFS's dean in 2009. During her tenure, Lancaster successfully launched two new master's programs, in Global Human Development and Asian Studies. She also raised funds for and oversaw the creation of the Georgetown Institute for Women, Peace and Security (GIWPS), hiring Ambassador Melanne Verveer, a Georgetown alumna and former director of the U.S. State Department's office for Global Women's Issues, as the institute's first director.

Joel Hellman, Ph.D.
2015–PRESENT

James Reardon-Anderson, Ph.D.
INTERIM DEAN 2014–2015

James Reardon-Anderson, who served as interim dean from 2014 to 2015, was the founding dean of the University's campus in Qatar, overseeing its establishment from 2005 to 2009 and subsequently returning for a second term from 2016 to 2017. A member of the Georgetown University faculty since 1985, he is currently a professor of history in the Georgetown University School of Foreign Service in Qatar. He also previously served as senior associate dean and director of the Georgetown University Master of Science in Foreign Service program.

Joel Hellman, who has served as the SFS dean since 2015, was previously the Chief Institutional Economist at the World Bank. Prior to that position, he served as director of the World Bank's Fragile and Conflict-Affected States department and was manager of the Governance and Public Sector Group in the South Asia region. He has taught in the political-science departments of both Harvard University and Columbia University, where he received his Ph.D.

Hellman has helped institute curricular changes to the SFS since becoming dean, particularly in the run-up to the School's centennial in 2019-2020. He oversaw the implementation of minors and the addition of a science requirement. He has hosted prominent practitioners for "coffee chats," informal discussions in the Dean's Office with small groups of students. The SFS has also seen the implementation of Centennial Labs under Hellman's tenure. These classes are meant to give students hands-on experience in topic areas like trade, drought in India, migration, and more, many including a travel component. He also oversaw the creation of the Center for Security and Emerging Technology, a research center focused on the security impacts of emerging technologies and providing nonpartisan analysis to the policy community. Their initial focus is on the effects of progress on artificial intelligence and advanced computing.

Chapter Two

The New Foreign Service

IN 1929, ON THE 10TH ANNIVERSARY OF THE FOUNDING of the School of Foreign Service, Secretary of State Frank Kellogg came to Georgetown to congratulate Father Walsh and his faculty on the high quality of foreign-service candidates the school was turning out. "The experience of the whole world has shown us the advisability and the necessity of trained personnel," said Kellogg.

The experience Kellogg was referring to was the conflict known as the Great War. Almost as soon as the war had begun in 1914, British diplomats and academics, joined by feminists in Europe and America, began agitating for a standing, multilateral diplomatic organization dedicated to peacemaking. By the end of the war, U.S. President Woodrow Wilson had put forward his own plan for such a body, which would take shape in 1920 as the League of Nations. Though Wilson could not convince the Congress to support the United States' participation in the League, the ideal of a peaceful world and the president's faith in international dialogue was widely shared in the country. Kellogg, a former U.S. senator from Minnesota and ambassador to Great Britain, would be awarded a share of the Nobel Peace Prize in 1921 for his part in the Kellogg-Briand Pact, a proposal issued with the foreign minister of France to outlaw war alto-

gether as a solution to international disagreements.

Kellogg's wishful pacifism — Adolf Hitler would be elected chancellor of Germany within three years — is often taken as a sign of the impotence of American diplomacy between the world wars. But as idealistic as the post-world war mood seems today, there was a determined, practical side to their hopes. Kellogg and others in Washington recognized that the U.S. diplomatic corps needed serious reform before it could serve as the vanguard for American ideals. At the time, statecraft was largely entrusted to business leaders and dyed-in-the-wool members of the elite. The practice of diplomacy likewise was regarded as an extension of the well-to-do social circles of Newport and Manhattan. At the State Department, then housed beside the White House in what is now known as the Old Executive Office Building, memorandums to staff drew distinctions between ordinary civil-service clerks and those addressed as "gentlemen." In his 10th-anniversary speech at Georgetown, Kellogg found it necessary to debunk the notion that "the principal duties of our secretaries and counselors ... were to attend social events."

To rebut these misconceptions, Kellogg pointed to the graduates in front of him and those who had preceded them. The young men who moved from Georgetown into the State Department were predominantly assigned to Latin America and the Far East, hardship posts, short on social niceties, that were considered suitable for unmarried young officers. Willard Beaulac (SFS'21), often referred to as the very first graduate because his name put him at the front of the Class of 1921's line to receive diplomas, quickly found himself serving as vice consul in Tampico, Mexico, then a bustling oil port. Before he was 30 years old, "Bo" Beaulac had filled consular posts in Honduras, Nicaragua, Haiti and Chile. He eventually became ambassador to Paraguay, Argentina and Colombia, and served

EARLY ADOPTER
Secretary of State Frank Kellogg, shown here at the north entrance to the Old Executive Office Building, believed in the necessity for the school.

as one of the last U.S. ambassadors to Cuba.

As the envoy to Havana in the mid-1950s, Beaulac had ample occasion to don white tie and tails. But in his 1951 memoir, *Career Ambassador*, he recounts tromping around the Latin American outback in the 1920s wearing a khaki shirt and trousers and with an automatic pistol on his belt. In 1924, during Honduras's second civil war, Beaulac brokered the surrender of the garrison town of Trujillo to the rebels who had it surrounded, then called in the U.S. Navy to enforce the arrangement and prevent a bloody takeover. After the telephone lines were cut in Trujillo, Beaulac walked to the town's dock amid looting and sporadic gunfire to see what had become of his request for military backup. "When we finally came to the street that leads to the bay," he wrote, "we saw the finest sight that I for one have been privileged to see. There was an American destroyer, with the Stars and Stripes gallantly waving from its stern, edging its way toward shore."

Beaulac's presence in Honduras, of course, was not entirely prompted by a Wilsonian vision of peace but in large part by the United States' growing economic interest in Central America. Puerto Castilla, where Beaulac was based, was the local headquarters of United Fruit, the multinational corporation whose land holdings across Caribbean-basin countries gave it an outsized role in regional politics. When Beaulac negotiated the surrender of Trujillo, he made sure that a United Fruit executive was at the table.

The new emphasis on diplomacy, then, was also designed to project and facilitate America's growing commercial power. Some 44 percent of the United States' international investments in 1924 went to Latin America, where American manufacturers had rushed in to replace the continent's European suppliers, who had been cut off from their customers by the

COMMERCIAL DIPLOMACY
Trujillo Bay today (left). Opposite, Ambassador Beaulac, center, during his time in the consular service in Mexico.

world war. After 1919, direct investment in Latin America began to outpace American capital flow to Europe.

Beaulac's career reflected this pivot, as did the careers of a number of his contemporaries. From the first two classes alone, James Picken went to Peru, Warren Ulrich to Mexico, and John Connelly, who would go on to have a long international legal career, began as a consul in Buenos Aires. Edwin Schoenreich was a consular official in Cuba and Bolivia. Richard Butrick, who would become the director general of the Foreign Service after the Second World War, began his climb in Chile in 1921.

The men in the field faced a grittier reality than the State Department's well-bred generalists, who were as likely to have been educated at Sciences-Po in Paris as at an American institution, were prepared for. The skills that got many early graduates through their initial postings, as the Navy veteran Beaulac's experience shows, were those they brought to Georgetown from their military service. Tampico, a stop for Beaulac in 1921 and the Class of 1924's Charles Gibney three years later, was a failing Mexican boomtown where American oil companies and their executives were regarded with growing hostility. In *Career Ambassador*, Beaulac recalls a trip made by mule to visit U.S. oilmen being held for ransom. At the very least, knowledge of weaponry and an ability to improvise under stress complemented a Georgetown education in these rough-and-tumble locations.

The diplomacy in these places could be prosaic. While serving in Guayaquil, Ecuador, in the mid-1920s, Butrick gained the release of an American merchant seaman who had been arrested while ashore. As he granted the seaman's freedom, the local governor mentioned that he had a pony he wanted to ship from the port by rail. "The railroad was built and controlled by an American company," Butrick told an interviewer for George-

"In 'Career Ambassador,' Beaulac recalls a trip made by mule to visit U.S. oilmen being held for ransom. At the very least, knowledge of weaponry and an ability to improvise under stress complemented a Georgetown education in these rough-and-tumble locations."

Madeleine Albright

WHEN I MOVED TO WASHINGTON IN 1968, I lived on 34th Street, NW, between N and O. I was still working on my Ph.D., and I often went to the Georgetown Library to do research and work, so I knew the place already. After the Carter administration ended, I was working with my boss, National Security Adviser Zbigniew Brzezinski, helping him get his book together, when [then SFS executive dean] Alan Goodman started talking to me about coming to Georgetown. Alan had raised money from the William H. Donner Foundation to hire a woman professor to encourage young women to join the School of Foreign Service and be interested in international relations generally. I was hired mainly as a way to show that this was now a coed school.

I had never taught before. I'd been on the Hill, working as chief legislative aide to Ed Muskie, and then I'd been at the White House. I loved the combination of being involved in politics and diplomacy and also being a professor. My father was a diplomat and an academic, so I thought it could work, and it did. I taught a course on executive-legislative relations and a course on Eastern European politics. I taught Modern Foreign Governments,

taking over from Jan Karski when he retired.

But I felt that what I should be doing was helping to train young women for foreign service. We were not just a school of international affairs generally, but foreign service, which is a coed business. I wanted to teach them how to be in partnership with men. When I was on the Hill, and later the White House, I was lucky because I had my credentials together just when people wanted a woman in a job. But I was often the only woman at the table. At times I'd stop myself from saying something because I worried I'd sound stupid, but then some man would say it, and everyone would think he was brilliant. I turned that into one of my mantras: Women have to learn to interrupt.

So I encouraged the women in my classes to interrupt. I did a lot of role-play, and I'd put women into roles they might not have, like Secretary of Defense. That became part of my teaching mechanism.

Because it was here in Washington, there was also a chance to have a public voice on things. There was the annual Leadership Seminar, where mid-level people from around the world would come to be immersed in what Washington was about. It created a real

LEARNING TO INTERRUPT
Hired 'to show that [SFS] was now a coed school,' Albright taught women to trust in what they had to say.

network — it was there that I first met Jaswant Singh, who later became Foreign Minister of India when I was Secretary of State. At the same time, I used to go to Eastern and Central Europe with a USIA program that sent experts abroad, to do research and keep myself up to date. Then there was the PBS show *Great Decisions*, which Peter Krogh was a part of, that would have policy discussions weekly on television. So there was an outward look to it.

Meanwhile, I kept up a political life. I love politics, and if you're teaching government, it makes sense. I was a foreign-policy adviser

I love politics, and if you're teaching government, it makes sense.

to Walter Mondale when he ran for president in 1984, and to Geraldine Ferraro, his vice presidential nominee. I would travel with her and fly back from where she was campaigning on Wednesdays to teach. In 1988 I worked for Dukakis and was in Boston when Bill Clinton, then the governor of Arkansas, arrived to brief Dukakis for the presidential debates. We obviously stayed in touch, and I was the first Clinton person to go to the White House in November of 1992 to help

with the transition for the National Security Council. Out of that, he asked me to go to the United Nations [as U.S. ambassador to the UN], and I had to stop teaching.

But I lived two blocks away and always had dinners at my house. In the early days it was for Georgetown people who wanted to talk about foreign policy but also wanted to know about politics — what could really be done in a political setting. Bob Lieber, chair of the Politics department, used to come by, among many others. In the '80s, when the Democrats were out of office, I used to cook for everyone, and we'd sit around and talk about things. But as Secretary, it was the academic discussions I missed, despite the fact that I was being briefed by the best of the best [at the State Department]. So I began having what I called "no-fault" dinners with a group of professors, where I could ask questions without anyone thinking I was looking for an answer to something immediate.

When I left the State Department, the School asked me to come back to teach, this time as an endowed professor. Before I'd left in the '80s, the school had already started to expand into business diplomacy, and the curriculum keeps adjusting to what international affairs is becoming — climate and public health — so that we are still training people to be everything they can be, in every part of the international system.

town's Foreign Affairs Oral History project. "I said, 'I will see what I can do about it.' So I arranged for the railroad to have his pony shipped up-country free of charge."

At the same time that Georgetown had begun providing professionally trained officers, modernization was coming to the State Department's strict but arcane hierarchy. In 1919, John Rogers, a Republican congressman from Massachusetts who had seen military service during the recent war, introduced his first bill aimed at restructuring State along the lines of the Navy. Rogers wanted to open its ranks to more candidates, in part by rationalizing its salary structure, and make the department generally more efficient.

At the time, the department's overseas personnel were divided into diplomatic secretaries and consular officers. The consuls were commerce-oriented and somewhat more professional than the diplomats, and only slighter better paid: Because the diplomatic service was the domain of the moneyed elite, salaries were abysmally low, and expenses for the cost of living abroad or for home leave were nonexistent. It was assumed that the secretaries came with their own funds. Some believed this situation was best. In place of any rigorous requirements for selecting diplomats, the pecuniary prerequisites of the job were considered a form of self-selection. William Castle, the ultramontane chief of the Bureau of Western European Affairs, resisted Rogers's reforms, declaring that "no man ... not possessed of a long income" should be allowed to be a diplomat.

Six years passed before Rogers, working with the like-minded chief of the Consular Bureau, Wilbur Carr, could push through all of his reforms. The capstone of his efforts, the 1924 Rogers Act, recommissioned all State Department employees serving overseas — 120 diplomatic secretaries and 521 consular officers — as foreign-service officers, to be paid not only equally but at higher rates, along with pensions and other financial support. A new Foreign Service exam was devised to standardize the criteria for admission.

In return, the new foreign-service officer was expected to think and behave like a professional. Ten military-like ranks were created and, as in the armed services, those not fit for promotion would be forced out. The new system, Rogers believed, would lay "the foundation for a thoroughly progressive, modern, and businesslike foreign service."

Rogers's revolution took years longer to take effect. Presidential prerogative meant that the most visible and desirable appointments went to those with political connections. For many lower posts, the State Department continued to rely on the Ivy League and wealthy families to furnish socially adept secretaries. The fact was that Father Walsh's new school, and those that followed Georgetown's lead, could not turn out enough graduates to fill the bulk of State's rapidly ex-

> "The fact was that Father Walsh's new school, and those that followed Georgetown's lead, could not turn out enough graduates to fill the bulk of State's rapidly expanding service. But those that Georgetown did provide were full of the modern, businesslike spirit of Rogers's reforms."

"Only in 1969, the year after the entire university became coed,
did the school drop its quota on female candidates:
Between 1953 and 1970, per the quota, only one woman could
be admitted to the school for every eight men."

panding service. But those that Georgetown did provide were full of the modern, businesslike spirit of Rogers's reforms.

One serious reform would have to wait until after the Second World War, when Georgetown would again help reshape not only the Foreign Service but agencies across the government.

In the mid-1940s, the School of Foreign Service had begun training dozens of women, apparently at the request of the Defense Department. Believing (correctly, according to recent studies) that women excel over men at learning other languages, the Pentagon had prevailed on Georgetown to make the foreign-language curriculum developed for Washington-area reservists and other military personnel available to women. In 1946, Anne S. Lawrence and Mary Alice Sheridan were awarded B.S.F.S. degrees from the School of Foreign Service, becoming the first women to receive diplomas from the school. (They were not the first to receive any degree from Georgetown; the university's nursing school had been graduating women exclusively since 1906, and in the early 1920s, nine nuns from the Visitation Convent on 35th Street Northwest were matriculated as graduate students.)

The language program, and the women who attended it, were a wartime oddity, however. Housed off-campus, as were its female students, it was a pale predecessor of the innovative Institute of Linguistics and Languages, known as

"Ling-Lang," founded in 1949 and based on the simultaneous translation system developed by its first head, Leon Dostert, for the Nuremberg war-crime trials. Nor were the women enrolled in the program typical undergraduates. One, Jesse Pearl Rice, was a U.S. Army lieutenant colonel and assistant director of the Women's Army Corps. When she arrived at Georgetown, she already held a B.A. from Converse College in South Carolina and a master's degree from Emory University in Atlanta, and had taught history at Georgia's Brenau College before enlisting in the women's corps at the outbreak of the war. (Rice went on to earn her history Ph.D. from Columbia shortly before her death in 1949.)

It would be another decade before the School of Foreign Service welcomed women as undergraduates, and only in 1969, the year after the entire university became coed, did the school drop its quota on female candidates: Between 1953 and 1970, per the quota, only one woman could be admitted to the school for every eight men.

As Georgetown and the wider academic world slowly opened to women, the Foreign Service itself retained a genteel institutional discrimination. It was assumed that young women would eventually marry and leave their careers to stay home. Taking her oral exam for the Foreign Service in 1968, Ruth Han-

LING-LANG
Leon Dostert, far left, outside of the Institute of Languages and Linguistics in 1953. Right, students in the Institute of Languages and Linguistics from the 1950 yearbook.

sen was bluntly asked about her marriage plans. "At that time I simply did not expect ever to get married. I expected to remain single and wanted a Foreign Service career," Hansen recalls in her oral history interview with the Association for Diplomatic Studies. "That was the answer I gave. . . . [W]hen they called me back in to tell me that I had not passed the exam, the one officer said that they were sorry that they couldn't admit me into the Foreign Service. But, he said, you're going on to Georgetown for graduate school; you'll probably marry a nice young man and you won't have to worry about a career."

Hansen did go on to attend the graduate program at the School of Foreign Service, from 1968 to 1970, followed by a 30-year State Department career that saw her serve as political officer in the Balkans, deputy director of Peacekeeping and Humanitarian Affairs, and director of the Policy Planning and Coordination Office.

Presuppositions about women's lack of career drive might have been self-fulfilling. As late as 1985, 22 percent of women in the Foreign Service held political positions, and 37 percent did consular jobs. By contrast, 41 percent of male Foreign Service officers were on the political side, and 16 percent were consuls. The consequences of the gender split became more apparent the higher one looked in the State Department hierarchy. Of those designated senior officers at State in 1985, only 3 percent were women.

But cracks in the predominantly male culture had begun to form even before the Allied forces landed on D-Day. State Department officials could see that, with the war's end, the United States would inherit a larger role in world affairs and that women would be needed in greater numbers to fill the swelling ranks of the Foreign Service. "The present ratio is about one in a thousand," the *New York Times* reported in March of 1944.

"The opening for women would be more than a demographic necessity; the acceptance of women in other countries was making the diplomatic world more welcoming."

"The career service numbers about 5,000, its women about five." That was about to change, as Nathaniel P. Davis, the State Department's chief of Foreign Service Personnel, told the *Times*. "When this war ends we will be short of personnel, at a time when we need a great increase." The opening for women would be more than a demographic necessity; the acceptance of women in other countries was making the diplomatic world more welcoming. "Except for the Moslem countries," Davis added, "prejudice against women in diplomatic posts is disappearing."

Coming less than eight years after the war's end, Georgetown's decision to admit women to the School of Foreign Service in 1953 was a significant step toward making gender equality possible at State. The fact that the university as a whole took nearly two decades to follow suit suggests that the appearance of women was not the result of any evolution in the administration's educational philosophy, but rather Father Walsh's ardent willingness to put his school in the Cold War fight. Walsh likely was responding to urgings from the same federal agencies that had depended on Georgetown to train women during the war.

The changes at Georgetown came as part of a wider recognition of women's skills at the State Department in the early '50s. The same year that the Walsh School began taking applications from women, President Eisenhower appointed Frances Willis ambassador to Switzerland, making her the first female career Foreign Service officer to become an ambassador. At the same time, State and other agencies were trying to

CEILING BROKEN
Barbara Hammes Sharood was among the first women to graduate SFS, in 1958 (left). Right, a student in Mechanized Education pictured in the 1953 yearbook.

Abba Schwartz

"THE TROUBLE IS THAT THE CONGRESS WANTS a closed society and you are trying to make it an open one," Secretary of State Dean Rusk told Abba Schwartz in March of 1966, according to Schwartz's memoir, *The Open Society*. Schwartz (SFS'36), a prominent adviser to Eleanor Roosevelt and John F. Kennedy and once identified as "the leading liberal at the State Department," had been pushed out of his post overseeing refugee policy. Whether Rusk's neat summation was true at the time, Schwartz's resignation soon became a measure of how well Americans, a dozen years after the end of the last House Un-American Activities Committee hearing, had moved on from McCarthyism.

Schwartz came to the School of Foreign Service from his hometown of Baltimore, and after graduating got his J.D. in 1939 from Harvard. It was there that he became an advocate for refugees fleeing Hitler's Third Reich in Eastern Europe. Still only 23 years old, he was granted an audience with President Franklin Roosevelt to voice his concerns. FDR, who saw the refugees' plight as "something for the missus," Schwartz recalled, referred him to the First Lady. Mrs. Roosevelt and Schwartz became friends. After the world war, Schwartz worked

for the International Refugee Organization and as special counsel for the Intergovernmental Committee for European Migration.

After returning to Washington in 1950 to practice immigration law, he kept up his political connections. He arranged for Eleanor Roosevelt to meet the young Jack Kennedy at the 1956 Democratic Convention in Chicago, to pitch Kennedy as a possible running mate for the presidential nominee, Adlai Stevenson. (Roosevelt passed, citing Kennedy's diffidence regarding McCarthy's red-baiting.) Four years later Schwartz brought the two together again in Hyde Park, and this time succeeded in prompting Mrs. Roosevelt to get behind JFK's own bid for president. With Kennedy in the White House, Schwartz was named Assistant Secretary of State for Security and Consular Affairs.

There was no little irony in Kennedy's pick for the post, from which Schwartz would oversee the Passport Office, the Visa Office, and the Office of Special Consular Services. President Eisenhower had created the position at the height of McCarthy's crusade, and its initial occupant had been Scott McLeod, "one of McCarthy's chief instruments for tyrannizing the State Department," as *Harper's* magazine later described him. Now Schwartz set about granting visas to applicants espousing a wide spectrum of political views, from a Japanese recipient of the Lenin Peace

STOLEN MEMORIES *Abba P. Schwartz, left, often served as the conscience of the United States on refugee matters. Here he examines a crate of gold and silver confiscated by Germans during World War II with Col. William G. Brey.*

Prize bound for a lecture tour to the right-wing African politician Moise Tshombe. He drafted legislation to get rid of immigration quotas.

When his department was reorganized while Schwartz was abroad, he resigned rather than take another unspecified post. While the reorganization was sold as part of a wider effort to streamline State, many took it as evidence of the "incredible political jungle" Washington remained in the wake of the red scare, in the words of one newspaper report. "The Abba Schwartz story," *The Washington Post* reported, "might well be headed: 'Joe McCarthy Rides Again.'"

If conservatives on the Hill had conspired to stop Schwartz, their effort backfired. A clampdown on visas and new passports for refugees that followed Schwartz's departure prompted an investigation into the Passport Office, and it was learned that the FBI had been spying on Americans who sympathized with Communism as they traveled in Europe and Asia. Senator Ted Kennedy declared, "The right to travel without harassment by our government is a fundamental right of American citizenship. I trust the Department will take every step necessary to see that our citizens can travel with the guarantee of privacy."

Schwartz wasn't daunted by his notoriety. After Cuba fell to Fidel Castro's rebels, he negotiated an agreement that allowed thousands of Cubans to come to the United States, and he later assisted in placing displaced people during the Vietnam War. He died in 1989 on his way to a meeting at the American embassy in Brussels.

broaden their candidate pools beyond the white Eastern elite characterized as "male, pale, and Yale."

Progress was slow. Many women found on entering the Foreign Service that they were shunted into administrative roles or directed toward the less prestigious consular side of embassy work. Nonetheless, by the turn of the 21st century, women were entering the Foreign Service at a higher rate than men. In 2005, 54 percent of the service were men — a 30-percentage-point drop in just 20 years. And while political appointees continue to outnumber career officers among female ambassadors, the ratio has steadily dropped over the past few decades. The presumption that women should not or cannot serve equally with men has effectively faded, according to Deborah McCarthy (MSFS'79), who earned a dual economics/foreign service master's degree from Georgetown in 1979 and went on to become ambassador to Lithuania.

Women's acceptance in the Foreign Service is certainly attributable to changing attitudes in society as a whole, but the government's use of Georgetown's coeds, particularly their perceived skill with languages, suggests they were more than symptoms of a larger phenomenon. The CIA won't discuss its hiring patterns, but anecdotal evidence suggests that the agency was glad to exploit the women at Georgetown. Lona Dwayne Sottile (MSFS'56) came to the SFS from Pomona College in California in 1954 after spending her junior year in Mexico City. Sometime during her two years at the School, says her daughter, Kathleen Nunnink, Sottile, who went by L.D., was recruited by the CIA. She was sent to El Salvador as an intelligence analyst, returning three years later to a job at CIA headquarters. Shortly afterward, Sottile married the dental graduate student she had met while at Georgetown and left the CIA.

Today Georgetown has continued to increase opportunities

"By the turn of the 21st century, women were entering the Foreign Service at a higher rate than men. In 2005, 54 percent of the service were men — a 30-percentage-point drop in just 20 years."

for all of its students by expanding its curriculum. The CIA's culture has long been seen as impenetrable for women, who have historically been pushed toward deskbound case-management positions, while men tend to become the front-line case officers. "I was told numerous times by HR, 'He's a man, he'll be able to handle the different sources'," says Michele Rigby Assad, a former CIA operative who earned her M.A. in Arab Studies in 2000.

Rigby Assad's hopes for a serious intelligence career were stymied until the tragedies of September 11, 2001. "It was challenging to be an Arab specialist before 9/11," says Rigby Assad. "On September 12, there weren't enough people in the world who knew about the Middle East." She was told that her background investigation, which had been on hold, was being resumed. Soon she was stationed in Iraq as a clandestine service officer. She credits the practical and thorough preparation she got at Georgetown. "It was such a deep dive into the Arab world," she says.

The university has consistently reached out to enrich the capabilities of the military and other defense agencies, notably by founding the National Security Studies program at the Pentagon in 1977. Robert Cardillo, director of the United States' National Geospatial-Intelligence Agency since 2014, was working as an imagery analyst for the Defense Intelligence Agency when he began classes for his master's degree at the Pentagon

in the fall of 1985. "You'd go down there around 5:30, after work, find the classroom and sit for the seminar," Cardillo recalls.

Interrogating suspected insurgents in Iraq may not be precisely what Frank Kellogg or Woodrow Wilson envisioned for the United States' engagement with the world. Certainly, no one would confuse the work of Georgetown's graduates today with effete social events. Georgetown has played no small part in helping realize Rogers's vision of professionalizing and democratizing government service, beyond the State Department to the CIA and other agencies he might not have imagined.

The professionalism and egalitarianism has come with no diminution of intellectual sophistication. Within the brief to produce capable foreign-service officers, the School of Foreign Service has been able to imbue its students with, as one graduate with a long career in the State Department put it, "a depth of understanding that others [in the Foreign Service] just don't have."

Some attribute the difference Georgetown has made to the moral foundation of the Jesuit ethic, or to a given class—Father Frank Winters's Ethics and International Relations course, Carroll Quigley's or Ulrich Aller's History of Political Theory or, most legendary, Carroll Quigley's required Development of Civilizations. Ambassador Edward Djerejian (SFS '66) credits above all a class in Shakespeare which, says the State Department's former Director of Near Eastern Affairs, "taught me the role of personality in politics and history." Georgetown, Djerejian says, informed his approach throughout his career. "When I got to a position of policy formation and influence," he says, "I realized the goal was to serve our country in the most interesting and dynamic way I can."

> "Within the brief to produce capable foreign-service officers, the School of Foreign Service has been able to imbue its students with 'a depth of understanding that others [in the Foreign Service] just don't have.'"

HIDDEN INFLUENCE Deborah Ann McCarthy (MSFS'79), below, negotiated drug interdiction agreements before becoming ambassador to Lithuania. Opposite, Michele Rigby Assad (MAAS'00) in her CIA years.

SFS-Q

The School as a Cultural Crossroad

WHEN PATRICK THEROS (SFS'63) FIRST FLEW into Doha, Qatar's capital, in 1963, the then low-lying city was barely distinguishable from the surrounding countryside. But even then the city had much to recommend it, says Theros, who visited the city often as a U.S. consular officer based in Riyadh, Saudi Arabia.

Theros spent much of the next 35 years in the Middle East, serving in Jordan, Syria, Lebanon, and the United Arab Emirates before rising to become political advisor to the commander-in-chief of the U.S. Central Command and deputy coordinator for counterterrorism. He ended his State Department career back in Doha, as the United States ambassador from 1996 to 1998.

But as Theros's tenure at the embassy was winding down, he opened a new chapter in his connection to Qatar, and his influence on the Middle East. In Theros's last year as U.S. ambassador, Qatar's emir, Sheikh Hamad bin Khalifa Al Thani, and Sheikha Moza bint Nasser discussed with him their plan to lure a major research university to Doha. The royals told Theros they wanted to establish in Qatar an institution to rival the prestigious American University in Beirut and the school of the same name in Cairo, and to provide healthy competition for Qatar University, which in two decades of existence had not distinguished itself.

With the support of her husband, who had declared himself the "Education Emir," Sheikha Moza became the driving force behind the effort, which would allow Qatari women, who were not granted the privilege of traveling outside the country, to get a first-rate education at home.

When Theros was called in to help with the problem, Sheikha Moza had already been turned down by two Ivy League universities about opening a Doha campus. Theros took her idea to Father Leo O'Donovan, then president of Georgetown University, with the same result. They got the same answer from the Ohio State University, the University of Illinois, and the University of Indiana, all leaders in the fields that most interested the Qataris: engineering, medicine, and business. All of them also said no.

"It was the Sheikha who saw what the solution was," says Theros. Discussions with the state universities had come apart because of

HIGH HONOR
Haroon Yasin (SFS'15) accepts his Queen's Young Leaders Award from Queen Elizabeth at Buckingham Palace in July 2018.

INTELLECTUAL OASIS
*The School of Foreign Service
in University City, Doha.*

SUCCESSFUL SCHOLARS
H.E. Sheikh Mohamed bin Hamad al Thani (SFS'09) is congratulated by his parents upon receiving his degree at the inaugural GU-Q Convocation in 2009 (left). This page, Dana Qarout (SFS'15), with other students at the student-led Justice in Palestine Week.

the hodgepodge of demands from faculty of the universities' various departments. "It turns out not all professors want the same things," Theros says. Negotiating with one faculty at a time, the Sheikha saw, would get around this obstacle. She decided to assemble a world-class university one department at a time.

The new strategy yielded an agreement with Weill-Cornell Medical College, which opened its building in the sector of Doha now known as Education City in 2001. Texas A&M University followed with an engineering school, Carnegie Mellon with computer science, and Virginia Commonwealth University with an art-and-design curriculum.

When the Sheikha came to Theros again in 2002 to inquire about a school for diplomatic training and international studies, the retired ambassador, who by then had joined the U.S. Qatar Business Council as president, took up the matter with Robert Gallucci, then dean of the School of Foreign Service.

Over the next three years, however, the

Jesuit university and the Muslim Qatari royals would come to a series of understandings about the financing of the school, the admission requirements, and the Catholic nature of the curriculum. The latter proved to be the most difficult part of the negotiation.

"At our first meeting, I told the Sheikha, 'This is not a match made in heaven,'" Gallucci recalls. "There are easier ways to get a school with a focus on international affairs."

The Sheikha was undeterred. "You think religion is important," she told Gallucci. "We think religion is important. That's what matters."

Both sides agreed that students on both campuses should receive the same degree and therefore the same education. For Georgetown, that meant requiring students from conservative Muslim homes to take The Problem of God, a class that stresses "the importance of promoting critical reflection on religious belief," according to the course catalog description.

The Sheikha's determination to bring Georgetown to Doha was instrumental. "I got along well with their negotiator, but I also knew that behind him was Sheikha Moza," recalls Gallucci. "When I was told, 'We can't give you this,' I knew that if I could get to Her Highness, life would be good."

In the fall of 2005, just three months after a final agreement was signed, the school opened with 18 students. In 2018, the student body totaled 288.

From the beginning those students have been unexpectedly diverse. The royal family "wanted to train their population to engage the world," says Brendan Hill, associate dean of student affairs

When Dean Gallucci told Qatar's Sheikha Moza bint Nasser that a Catholic university and her Muslim nation was "not a match made in heaven, the Sheikha replied ,"You think religion is important. We think religion is important. That's what matters."

of SFS-Q and instructor in Doha since 2009. "What they soon saw was that the school would expose Qataris to people all over the world."

Forty-four nationalities are now represented at the school, which draws widely from the Gulf region and beyond. "The student body is divided into equal thirds," says Hill. "There are longtime expat families, international students from as far away as Korea and Costa Rica, and Qataris."

That mix of Western and Eastern, middle-class and oil-wealth elite, male and female, has challenged the Qatari students' culturally. "They've been educated in Western schools, but it's often their first time in a gender-integrated place," says Hill.

But it is bringing together people to discuss ideas, including scientific concepts and the history of the West, that has the greatest potential to change minds. The microcosm of cultures— as Hill points out, "every empire is represented in class"—has become "a space where otherwise difficult issues can be discussed."

SFS-Q has seen the Sheikha's dream of introducing young Qataris to the world realized. These include the Qatari royals, such as the current emir's heir and deputy emir, Abdulla bin Hamad Al Thani, who graduated in 2010 and was recently made chairman of the board of directors of the state-owned energy company Qatar Petroleum, and Sheikh Mohamad bin Hamad Al Thani (SFS '09), who chaired the committee that brought the 2022 World Cup to Qatar and is now directing the effort to build out the infrastructure for the event.

BY THE NUMBERS

AS OF FALL 2018:

288

Total number of enrolled students, representing
44 NATIONALITIES

FORTY-FIVE

Full-time faculty members

6:1   STUDENT TO FACULTY RATIO

TWENTY-FIVE +

Student clubs, athletic teams and activities

LIBRARY HOLDINGS

Printed resources: 90,060
Electronic resources:

1,471,055

FORTY-ONE %

Graduates have earned or are working toward a Ph.D., Master's or Law degree

439

Total number of graduates, representing
51 NATIONALITIES

47   *Community courses offered between the years 2015–2018*

EMPLOYMENT SECTORS FOR SFS-Q GRADUATES

Art/culture, business/consulting, diplomacy, government/law, education, energy, engineering, events/sports, finance, healthcare, tourism/hospitality, museums, public relations/media, research, technology

SFS-Q

The school has also succeeded in its goal of educating women from Qatar and the Muslim world, who otherwise often lack an entree to the wider world.

Dana Khalid Al-Anzy (SFS'17) has become known for her advocacy and service through the children's empowerment organization Education Above All, which she represented at the United Nations General Assembly while still a student. Two years earlier, Dana Qarout (SFS'15), a Palestinian Jordanian, graduated from SFS and immediately joined the Queen Rania Foundation in Amman to work on educating the refugee population in Jordan.

Not least, the Doha campus has expanded on Georgetown's already international character. "It has helped us become a truly global university," says Georgetown President John J. DeGioia, "a university that builds bridges among individuals, countries and cultures and that shapes young men and women to bring this understanding to every field of inquiry."

ROYAL AGREEMENT
Georgetown President John J. DeGioia and H.H. Sheikha Moza bint Nasser at the signing ceremony on May 17, 2005 for the agreement between Georgetown University and the Qatar Foundation to open a campus for the School of Foreign Service in Qatar.

09

10

11

12

ALUMNI

Georgetown Leadership Seminar Fellows

1. Helle Degn (GLS'85), Denmark, former Member of Parliament and former Minister for Development Cooperation; **2. José Manuel Barroso** (GLS'98), Portugal, former President of the European Commission, former Prime Minister; **3. Jens Stoltenberg** (GLS'88), Norway, Secretary General of NATO, former Prime Minister; **4. Mary Collins** (GLS'87), Canada, former Associate Minister of National Defence; former Minister responsible for the Status of Women; **5. Issa Konfourou** (GLS'15), Mali, Permanent Representative and Ambassador to United Nations; **6. Poonam Mahajan** (GLS'15), India, Member of Parliament; **7. Mina Al-Oraibi** (GLS'12), Iraq and United Kingdom, Editor-in-Chief of *The National*, **8. César Gaviria Trujillo** (GLS'84), Colombia, former President, former Secretary General of the Organization of American States, former National Director of the Liberal Party; **9. Michael Hayden** (GLS'99), General (retired), United States Air Force, former Director of the National Security Agency, former Director of the Central Intelligence Agency; **10. Roberto Dañino** (GLS'83), Peru, former Prime Minister, former Peruvian Ambassador to the United States and former Senior Vice President and General Counsel of the World Bank; **11. Olena Zerkal** (GLS'18), Ukraine, Deputy Foreign Minister; **12. Mahmoud Mohieldin** (GLS'03), Egypt, Senior Vice President of the World Bank for the '30 Development Agenda, United Nations Relations, and Partnerships

Ministers

1. **Taro Kono** (SFS'86), Foreign Minister of Japan; 2. **Ambassador Kasit Piromya** (SFS'68), former Foreign Minister of Thailand; 3. **David Y.L. Lin (**MSFS'90), former Minister of Foreign Affairs of the Republic of China (Taiwan); 4. **Kristjen Nielsen** (SFS'94) former Secretary of Homeland Security; 5. **H.H. Sheikh Abdullah bin Hamad Al-Thani** (SFS'10), Deputy Emir of Qatar; 6. **Nasser Judeh** (SFS'83), former Foreign Minister of Jordan; 7. **Ambassador Bruno Stagno Ugarte** (SFS'91), former Foreign Minister of Costa Rica; 8. **Wang Yi** (ISD Associate 1997–'98), Minister of Foreign Affairs of the People's Republic of China

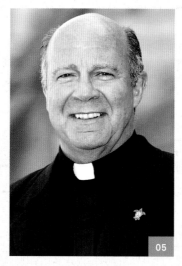

Education

1. **B. Joseph White** (SFS'69), President Emeritus, University of Illinois; 2. **Debora Spar** (SFS'84), former President, Barnard College; 3. **Kaya Henderson** (SFS'92), former Chancellor of DC Public Schools; 4. **Carmen Twillie Ambar** (SFS'90), President, Oberlin College; 5. **Lawrence Biondi, S.J.** (MSFS'66), President Emeritus, St. Louis University

Chapter Three

SFS and the Cold War

F
OR NEARLY HALF OF THE SCHOOL OF FOREIGN SER-
VICE'S HUNDRED years of existence, the United States
was engaged in the Cold War struggle against communism. If one counts Father Walsh's visceral antipathy toward the Soviet Union, which was spurred by his visit
to Russia in 1923, anti-communism was a theme at the School of
Foreign Service for more than 60 years. For the graduates who
entered the Foreign Service, the Cold War was never an abstract
conflict of ideologies. In a war of influence, embassies in Europe,
Latin America and Africa were often the front line, and Georgetown students were trained to serve as ground troops.

The concerns that sent the first graduates of the School of
Foreign Service to Tampico, Mexico, and Venezuela as vice consuls to secure oil concessions were the same that gave birth to the
Cold War. In the 1920s, oil was already the world's key strategic
commodity. Oil had fueled the tanks and fighter planes that had
won the recent world war—"The Allies floated to victory on a
wave of oil," as the British minister Lord Curzon intoned in 1918—
and as World War II began, controlling the globe's oil fields was
the first order of business for the Western powers.

Five years later, at the dawn of the Cold War, oil was at
the center of the first, bloodless skirmish between the United
States and the Soviet Union. It was won through the ingenuity
of a 27-year-old SFS graduate named Robert Rossow (SFS'39).

After Hitler invaded Russia in the summer of 1941, Stalin

PIVOT POINT
With the surrender of
Japan in September 1945
— signed in ceremonies
aboard the *USS Missouri*
and celebrated in Times
Square, right — the
mission of the Foreign
Service and the character
of the SFS education
would change profoundly.

COLD WARRIOR
In 1941, Robert Rossow Jr., shown with wife, Kathryn, and presenting his credentials in Vancouver, was a vice-consul in British Columbia. By the end of the Second World War, he was facing the Soviets in Iran.

joined with his newfound allies Britain and the United States in occupying Iran, with the object of keeping the country's oil supply out of Nazi hands. After the war, it was agreed, the three countries would withdraw and in the meantime no oil concessions would be granted to any of the occupying powers.

Months after V-J Day, however, Russian troops were still lingering in northern Iran, claiming to be protecting a fledgling democratic republic in Azerbaijan. As the March 1946 deadline for withdrawal neared and Iran and its Western allies cried foul, it became clear that Stalin was maneuvering "for the privilege of exploiting oil," as *The New York Times* put it in a front-page article on the crisis. It was feared that Stalin intended to take Tehran. The closest American observer, the longtime consul in Tabriz, tried to allay Washington's fears, sending cables reassuring his bosses that "peace and tranquility reign."

President Truman and Secretary of State Edward Stettinius were unconvinced, and, frustrated by the vague reports coming out of Tabriz, the small Iranian city in the middle of the Soviet sector, sent Robert Rossow to take a look. Though not of the Great War generation, Rossow was very much in the pre-World War II Georgetown mold.

Rossow had grown up on the grounds of Culver Academy, a military preparatory school in northern Indiana, where his father was an instructor and director of the Black Horse Troop, a locally famous cavalry unit. According to Rossow's son, Robert Rossow III, a retired U.S. Army lieutenant colonel, Rossow initially enrolled at Columbia University, but after being jilted by a fellow student decided to transfer to Georgetown and pursue a career in foreign service, a notion he'd gotten after meeting Father Walsh at the University of Notre Dame some years earlier. He did well at Georgetown, where he edited the Foreign Service Log and won the Casey Medal and the Jean

"At the dawn of the Cold War, oil was at the center of the first, bloodless skirmish between the United States and the Soviet Union. It was won through the ingenuity of a 27-year-old SFS graduate named Robert Rossow."

Labat Medal for excellence in French. Graduating in June of 1939 at the age of 20, he took the Foreign Service exam and, while he waited to be called up, belatedly accepted a commission in the U.S. Army that had come with his diploma from Culver Academy. The Army sent him to Fort Knox, where as a cavalry officer he was trained in tank warfare.

When the Japanese bombed Pearl Harbor, Rossow was a vice consul in Panama. Reading *The Washington Post*, which was included in the diplomatic pouch, Rossow was incensed by a story accusing Foreign Service officers of sitting out the war in embassies far from the combat zone. In fact, due to the State Department's increased wartime needs, Foreign Service officers were rarely permitted to leave in order to join the armed forces, but Rossow successfully resigned and asked to be reunited with his tank division, deployed in North Africa. He was told to report instead in a plain Army uniform without insignia to an office in Washington, where he was inducted into the Office of Strategic Services, the precursor to the Central Intelligence Agency. His training took place in Washington and in "a mansion up the Hudson River," his son recounts, "where he was instructed in, among other things, picking locks by an expert faculty

from nearby Sing Sing who were doing their patriotic duty."

At the end of the war, Rossow returned to the Foreign Service. At the time, President Truman was growing dissatisfied with the quality of information coming from Iran, and it was determined that a new vice consul was needed. Given his skills, Rossow was sent to Tabriz and ordered "to tell us what the hell was going on," according to family lore. Later accounts of Rossow's adventure in Tabriz make much of his ability, gained at Fort Knox, to recognize the headings of Soviet tanks by the tread marks in the sand, and even his careful observation of "horses' tracks, droppings, and other signs." But Rossow's own telegrams, while detailing troop movements by various means, show that the Soviets' intentions would have been abundantly clear to anyone watching the railroad station in Tabriz. On March 3, Rossow wrote, "50 Soviet trucks laden with supplies, mainly ammunition, departed Tabriz toward Iran." More than 100 tanks followed the next evening, even as dozens more appeared in Tabriz by train. At the end of March, Rossow, listening on short-wave radio on the consulate roof, heard Russian Foreign Minister Andrei Gromyko deny that the Soviets were on the march. "As these words came over the short-wave," Rossow later wrote, "a column of 18 armored half-tracks that had just been unloaded rumbled past on their way to the tank park."

With Rossow's telegrams and maps in hand (received and translated for the White House by Harold Minor (SFS'27), then chief of the Division of Near Eastern Affairs and a former Iran hand himself), the United States called the Soviets' bluff and ultimately forced them to withdraw their troops. With his military removed, Stalin lost his leverage to demand oil concessions, and the Iranian government quickly abrogated the agreement it had been pressured into signing. Not long afterward, the United States made its own deal for Iranian oil. Stalin was infuriated.

RED HANDED
Harold Minor, left, reported Rossow's intelligence on Soviet troop movements. Opposite, the Red Army entering Tabriz on August 30, 1941.

Alexander Graf Lambsdorff

ALEXANDER GRAF LAMBSDORFF'S (MSFS'92) name and title—the "Graf" identifies him as a German nobleman equivalent to a British earl, and he is also Baron von Wenge—might suit the 19th-century European elite's diplomatic circles better than those of the 21st century. The Lambsdorffs have been a prominent family in the German states since the Thirty Years' War in the 1600s and joined the ranks of nobility after Lambsdorff's forebears rendered distinguished military service in 1817. His political pedigree is also sterling: Lambsdorff's father, a journalist-turned-diplomat, was Germany's first ambassador to Latvia after the fall of the Soviet Union and later ambassador to Czechoslovakia. Lambsdorff's uncle Otto was an economics minister in the Free Democratic Party government of the late 1970s and early '80s.

Lambsdorff, who joined the Free Democrats as a matter of course in his twenties, betrays little of his patrimony: Urbane and fast-talking, he has a knack for releasing disarming sound bites and sometimes-profane tweets on Twitter. Whether speaking for his pro-Europe party's impatience with Brexit or articulating its nuanced immigration policy, Lambsdorff comes across as an assured politician whose lineage is secondary to his training.

A crucial part of that preparation came during his two years at the School of Foreign Service, where he arrived in 1991 as a Fulbright scholar after getting his undergraduate degree in Germany. It was an unnerving time to be away from home. Europe, whose polity was based on being cleaved in two for the entirety of Lambsdorff's life, was now atomizing and reforming. By the time he returned, the two

Lambsdorff projects optimism, energy and open-mindedness about world affairs, Europe, and its relationship with the United States.

Germanys were faced with the challenge of becoming a single nation even as other regions had taken advantage of newfound freedoms to declare independence. "We had to relearn the world around us," Lambsdorff told MSFS recipients at their graduation ceremony in 2012.

Lambsdorff also imbibed less tangible lessons on campus and in America as a whole, particularly, he has said, in the class on U.S.–Soviet relations taught by Madeleine Albright. With Clarence Thomas's confirmation hearings and Anita Hill's testimony dominating political discussion, Albright invited the whole class for dinner at her home to discuss sexual harassment. For someone who had grown up in the stricter environment of European schools, Albright's class was a chance to learn beyond the bounds of the classroom and experience an open-mindedness he had not known in Germany.

With his MSFS degree, with a concentration on trade and economics, which he had paired with a master's degree in the history department in Modern European History, not to mention his family background, Lambsdorff was a made-to-order candidate for Germany's sometimes-staid foreign service. But after a few years in the agency's policy shop and a stint as an embassy press officer that brought him back to Washington, Lambsdorff developed a taste for retail politics: He lost a local race in his home state in 2000, then won a seat in the European Parliament four years later.

When the Free Democrats' leader in Brussels fell prey to a résumé scandal in 2011, Lambsdorff was named chief and eventually became a vice-president of the parliament, a post he kept for the next seven years.

As Lambsdorff prospered in Brussels, his family's political home, the Free Democrats,

OPINION LEADER
*Lambsdorff speaking
in Berlin in 2011.*

had fallen on increasingly hard times. One of Germany's oldest political parties, and the long-reigning Christian Democratic Union's go-to partners in forming governments, the Free Democrats by 2013 had fallen so low in the polls they had dropped out of the lower house of the Bundestag. That year the party was taken over by Christian Lindner, who quickly turned its fortunes around by appealing to business and educated liberals—a profile made to order for Lambsdorff, who stood for a seat representing Bonn in the general election in 2017. He became one of 80 members of the Bundestag elected from the resurgent FDP and the party's spokesman for foreign affairs and Europe issues.

In his speeches on even the dreariest days in legislative forums, and in his readily offered opinions to the press, Lambsdorff projects optimism, energy, and open-mindedness about world affairs, Europe, and its relationship with the United States. A firm believer in the power of grassroots democracy, he has been quick to work in support of it as an election observer in Africa. At home he has shown enthusiasm for innovation and assaulting barriers that might slow Germany's pace. To the horror of some of his conservative colleagues, he not long ago advocated the adoption of English as an official language of the country—of which he leaves no doubt he is a committed citizen—to better attract the highly educated immigrants that he (and the Free Democrats) believe Europe's largest economy will need to sustain itself for the rest of the 21st century.

"One may fairly say that the Cold War began on March 4, 1946," Rossow wrote in his account of the crisis, citing the date of his first telegrams back to Washington. "Though not a shot was fired, the Battle of Azerbaijan was as significant in its outcome as Bunker Hill, Bull Run, or the Battle of the Marne."

In the years that followed, communism seemed to be advancing everywhere in the world, from China and the distant islands of Indonesia and Malaysia to Cuba, just off the coast of the United States. It was propelled in part by monolithic bureaucratic states such as the Soviet Union and, eventually, China's nationalist guerrilla movements and cultic Maoist insurgencies. The U.S. government's response was as various as the threat, and much of the work of containing communism involved economic support and development, educational exchange, and other inducements suited to the skills that Georgetown's diplomats were taught. In some places, ambassadors and their staffs exercised their sway by defending democratic principles. As U.S. ambassador to Malaya (now Malaysia) from 1961 to 1964, SFS graduate Charles Baldwin (SFS'26) "saw our role as bolstering democracy and all that it stood for against communism," says his son, C. Stephen Baldwin. A tall, dignified man reminiscent of British Prime Minister Anthony Eden, he was often invited to speak to large crowds of Malayans. "He spoke marvelously well," the younger Baldwin says, and inspired the locals to see the United States as a place of honor and good will. "He represented a kind of uncompromising Americanness."

On the other end of the scale were the proxy wars fought in Greece, Southeast Asia, Afghanistan, and Central America, occasions when the Cold War heated up and the Foreign Service was often drawn into, or at least close to, the battles.

The career of Michael Cotter (SFS'65), who came to Georgetown in 1961 from Madison, Wisconsin, and ended as ambassador

THEORIST OF
REALPOLITIK
Henry Kissinger speaking
at a press conference in
November 1975, shortly
after leaving his role
as national security
adviser. He would remain
as secretary of state
until 1977, when he
came to Georgetown.

to Turkmenistan in 1998, shows the range of the typical Foreign Service officer's Cold War engagement. After graduating in 1965 and taking the Foreign Service exam, he attended law school before joining the A-100 class of 1968. An earlier back operation had disqualified him from the draft, but upon entering the Foreign Service he was sent to Vietnam as part of an aid program known as CORDS (Civilian Operations and Revolutionary Development Support), designed to pacify Vietnamese civilians who might otherwise be recruited to help the Viet Cong.

Though his assignment would chiefly involve conducting surveys of villages in the Mekong Delta and aiding local families by distributing building materials and food and improving farmers' agricultural practices, Cotter spent his first weeks in the Foreign Service preparing to enter a war zone. "Our training included off-sites at Fort Bragg for weapon familiarization and at a remote site in Virginia," Cotter wrote in an article for the website American Diplomacy, "where we played a very realistic game [that] literally involved all of the rooms and other facilities of a large conference site and included simulated ambushes. Students played the parts of South Vietnamese villagers, American advisors, and Viet Cong." These war games were followed by 10 months of study of the Vietnamese language at the Foreign Service Institute in Rosslyn.

Once in Vietnam, Cotter asked to be assigned to the Mekong Delta, choosing a post that would allow him to interact with Vietnamese instead of other Americans. Besides coordinating projects sponsored by the United States Agency for International Development (USAID), he toured the villages in his district to interview and assess the feelings of the local population and prepared periodic "Hamlet Evaluation System" reports. While his data was useful to the war effort, Cotter takes pride in his agricultural mission. The last time he visited the area, he said in a recent interview, he cited the diversity in the local pig population as evidence that his tenure had perhaps opened local farmers' minds to different, more productive breeds.

As the war wound down, Cotter was sent to Bolivia, where a few months earlier Che Guevara, a hero of the Cuban revolution who was leading a small rebel force in the Bolivian mountains, had been captured (reportedly with help from CIA operatives) and killed. Not long before, the Bolivians had kicked out the Peace Corps. The primary role of the U.S. embassy was to support anti-Communist sentiment and shore up the government, in part through development programs of the kind he'd been pushing in Vietnam. "You were very conscious that you were fighting the Cold War," says Cotter. "If you wanted money for [aid programs]," he said in a recent

"I was awakened from a nap by shooting.
I looked outside to see tracers going back and forth
across the square, in front of the residence.
People were firing from and at the ministry of defense."

— MICHAEL COTTER (SFS'65)

interview, "you had to put it in a Cold War context."

Not that the global tug-of-war between the Communists and the free world was ever distant. In the early 1970s, President Juan Jose Torres, a leftist military officer, had replaced Rene Barrientos, the man who had ordered Guevara's execution. A force led by rightist military officers fought for Torres's ouster during much of Cotter's tenure in Bolivia. One afternoon, Cotter recalled, "I was awakened from a nap by shooting. I looked outside to see tracers going back and forth across the square, in front of the residence. People were firing from and at the ministry of defense." The rebellion had reached the capital, La Paz. "I was sitting there in the ambassador's residence all by myself," Cotter recalls, "hearing more firing closer than I had heard in 18 months in Vietnam."

As the Cold War wore on and political activism that had been focused on Vietnam shifted against U.S. support of strongmen in Latin America, Africa, and other places in the developing world, ambivalence grew in the United States about a single-minded anti-Communist foreign policy. The Nixon administration's detente initiative, aimed at warming relations with the Soviet Union, caused Americans to further question the policy of propping up dictators at a high cost to our credibility as a beacon of democracy. Further punctured by Nixon's toppling over Watergate, American confidence abroad and at home had sunk to a point that the realpolitik that had been a hallmark of Henry Kissinger's reign at State under Nixon and Ford was no longer sustainable. Congress had already begun to debate the need to integrate human rights into U.S. foreign policy, but after the election of Jimmy Carter to the White House in 1976, human rights became an official concern of American foreign policy.

The change was evident to Michael Cotter after just a three-year absence from South America. After two years in other posts, Cotter arrived in Quito, Ecuador, as the U.S. embassy's political-military officer in 1976. Six months earlier, a military junta had overthrown Ecuador's populist President Assad Bucaram. During his previous tour in Latin America, Cotter recalled, "our major concern was helping to shore up anti-Communist regimes. We weren't particularly interested in looking beyond that." This time, he says, the embassy, under orders from Washington, pressured the junta to restore democracy. "We were insisting they return power to a democratic government within three years, and they did."

When Ronald Reagan was elected in 1980, Secretary of State Al Haig continued to make human rights a factor in foreign affairs, at least on paper: Cotter says the Reagan State Department required more extensive, formalized reporting on human-rights violations than had the Carter White House.

How to advocate for democratic principles and human rights through foreign policy was often clearer with our Communist adversaries than with our allies. The 1973 Helsinki Accords, an agreement signed by some 35 Western European and Eastern bloc countries, included affirmations of respect for human rights and equality before the law and became a tool for urging the Soviets and their satellites to improve their treatment of dissidents.

> "The Helsinki Accords really laid the groundwork for American diplomats to pay more attention to human rights as yet another avenue of influence."
> — STEPHEN MULL (SFS '80)

Georgetown was at the center of the debate in the academy and no less so as it took shape on the ground in Europe, Africa, and Latin America. "The Helsinki Accords really laid the groundwork for American diplomats to pay more attention to human rights as yet another avenue of influence," says Stephen Mull (SFS'80), who attended the School of Foreign Service in the late 1970s before going to Poland as a junior Foreign Service officer in 1982. That year, Mull says, the leader of the dissident group Confederation for an Independent Poland, Leszek Moczulski, was put on trial for plotting to overthrow the country's Communist government. "I was instructed by Washington to try to get into the courtroom clutching a copy of the Helsinki accords and declare the proceedings

a violation of its principles." (The effort failed. "The guards essentially told me, 'Get out of here, kid,' " Mull recalls.)

At the same time, our dealings with Philippine strongman Ferdinand Marcos and Chilean dictator Augusto Pinochet were more nuanced, in part under the influence of a former School of Foreign Service political-science professor named Jeane Kirkpatrick.

A lifelong Democrat, Kirkpatrick came to Georgetown in 1967 and at first made her mark with her pioneering research on the place of women in American politics. As the '70s progressed, Kirkpatrick became politically involved herself. Soured on the Democrats after their disastrous choice of George McGovern to run against Richard Nixon in 1972, Kirkpatrick began her turn toward neoconservatism. By the latter part of the decade, she had established herself as a severe critic of Jimmy Carter's foreign policy. In her 1979 article "Dictatorships and Double Standards," published in *Commentary* magazine, Kirkpatrick argued that Carter's emphasis on human rights should not be applied uniformly. Old-school military dictators were a lesser evil than revolutionary socialists, she wrote, because they "do not disturb the habitual rhythms of work and leisure, habitual places of residence, habitual patterns of family and personal relations." Communists, on the other hand, are bent on remaking society, Kirkpatrick maintained, and therefore create greater disruption and misery.

After "Dictatorships and Double Standards" appeared, Ronald Reagan invited Kirkpatrick to join his presidential campaign as a foreign affairs advisor. Following Reagan's victory in the 1980 election, Kirkpatrick was named ambassador to the United Nations.

The School of Foreign Service was doubly represented in the Reagan White House, the other party being former Secretary of State and Nixon national-security advisor Henry Kissinger. In 1977, Dean Peter Krogh invited Kissinger to make

PUSHING BACK
Jeane Kirkpatrick made her mark with an argument that military dictators like President Ferdinand Marcos of the Philippines, shown with his wife, Imelda, in 1969, deserved more leniency than Communists.

QUEEN OF THE HILL
Former U.S. ambassador to the UN and Georgetown professor Jeane Kirkpatrick addresses the crowd at the "Salute to Georgetown" gala, opening the university's bicentennial celebrations in 1988.

Arms Control and Nonproliferation

WHEN THE SECRETARY-GENERAL OF THE United Nations, António Guterres, told Izumi Nakamitsu (MSFS'89) in March of 2017 that he planned to name the career UN staffer Under-Secretary-General and High Representative for Disarmament Affairs, Nakamitsu's immediate response was that she was no expert on disarmament or arms control.

Then again, Nakamitsu quickly points out, she can't claim any particular expertise. "I'm one of a few, very rare UN officials who have done so many things," she says—which is precisely what Guterres was looking for. "I don't want an expert," the Secretary-General told Nikamitsu. "I want someone who understands everything else."

The work of nuclear nonproliferation and other forms of arms control—in her post, Nakamitsu handles everything from the Iran nuclear deal to the regulation of handguns—demands a generalist. As the Iran nuclear deal has shown, technical knowledge, though essential when negotiating the fine points of uranium refinement or missile systems, is often not as crucial in nonproliferation and arms-control issues as familiarity with politics, geopolitical power struggles, and peacemaking. "Disarmament is actually closely related to war and to security issues," says Nakamitsu, now the highest-ranking Japanese official in the UN's history.

Seen in that light, there is an undeniable logic to Nakamitsu's involvement in disarmament. Her first job with the UN, as a junior program officer after earning her MSFS, took her to Turkey during the first Gulf War, where she aided refugees fleeing the conflict. Since then she has directed peacekeeping operations for the UN's Asia and Middle East division and served as Assistant Secretary-General for Crisis Response at the UN Development Program. In the 2000s, she took a nearly 10-year hiatus from the UN after marrying her husband, a Swedish diplomat, during which she worked for a democracy-assistance organization based in Stockholm and taught international relations at Hitotsubashi University in Tokyo.

War and security concerns also paved the way for Joseph Cirincione (MSFS'83) to lead the Ploughshares Fund, the world's largest nuclear-security foundation. First, though, the onetime Vietnam War protester took a decade-long tour as a community organizer in Boston, where his primary concern was fighting evictions in the city's depressed neighborhoods. His focus returned to the international scene in the first summer of Ronald Reagan's presidency, when American jets shot down two Libyan jets over the Mediterranean. "I thought the world was going to war," Cirincione recalls. "This superseded the concerns of community development. I wanted to make a difference. I wanted to stop that conflict."

His first step was to enroll in the MSFS program at the School of Foreign Service to shore up his knowledge of international affairs.

"The goal was to be a generalist, someone who knew a lot about foreign policy," he says.

His second was to infiltrate the conservative foreign-affairs establishment itself. "In my second semester, I answered an index card on a bulletin board to be a teaching assistant for an SFS professor, the late W. Scott Thompson." When Thompson, who had served as an assistant secretary of defense under President Ford, joined the Reagan administration as assistant director of the U.S. Information Agency in 1982, Cirincione went along. "I wanted to learn how these guys thought," he says. He ended up on an interagency working group on Central America, serving with a charismatic Marine lieutenant colonel named Oliver North.

He left government to join a think-tank-sponsored project that brought journalists into Central America to promote understanding between Americans and the countries where the United States had become actively engaged in local civil wars—Nicaragua and Honduras. When the project ended, he was hired as a national-security analyst on Capitol Hill, developing missile-defense policy for the House Armed Services Committee as Reagan's Strategic Defense Initiative—"Star Wars"—got under way. In 1993, he joined the Henry Stimson Center as a nuclear-nonproliferation expert, later jumping to the Carnegie Endowment for Peace and the Center for American Progress, where he was vice-president for international security and policy. Cirincione was named president of the Ploughshares Fund in 2008.

Cirincione's community organizing still

shapes how he does his job at Ploughshares. "We don't just raise money and give it to people with good ideas," he says. "We link them up with others and provide a network where they can coordinate their activities with other advocates and experts. We organize them toward common strategic objectives."

Similarly, Izumi Nakamitsu finds that the broad range of concerns that got her into disarmament still serve her work at the UN. She first came to the United States as an exchange student at Hope College in Michigan in the mid-1980s. At the end of that program, her American diplomacy professor suggested she try an internship on the Hill with Colorado Representative Pat Schroeder. For a young woman accustomed to Japan's male-dominated society, Schroeder, who had fought off being called "Little Patsy" when she was elected in the early '70s, proved an inspiration. Visiting a Japanese friend at Georgetown, Nakamitsu decided to stay for her master's.

The theory she learned at Georgetown has been an important tool as she has moved through the UN system. "You are thrown into all sorts of different phenomena," she says. "What helps you generalize and conceptualize the challenges is the theory."

But Nakamitsu says that in her latest role for the UN she has also been charged with taking disarmament out of the conference room to save lives. The reality of gender discrimination that helped convince Nakamitsu to make her career outside Japan has resurfaced as a theme in this pursuit. "Disarmament has a huge impact on gender roles," she points out. "When small arms are not properly regulated or managed in a conflict area, it has a very sharp impact on gender violence. The statistics clearly show that properly managing the instruments of war really benefits women very directly."

Wide-ranging experience is not an absolute prerequisite for anyone interested in the nonproliferation of nuclear weapons. Catherine Dill (SFS'09) became fascinated with the subject when, in her senior year at Georgetown, the Southern Californian took a course in the Security Studies program in nonproliferation with Edward Ifft, a former deputy director of the State Department's On-Site Inspection Agency. For Dill, who was raised Catholic and had a firm foundation in the Church's tradition of the Just War Doctrine, Ifft's class "linked up with what I knew about just-war theory. There was always a big emphasis for me on social justice."

Dill has gone on to further study conflict resolution at the graduate level and is a contributor to the anti-proliferation blog Atomic Wonk. Though she doesn't have the breadth of experience of her fellow alumni in the disarmament field, Dill is motivated by the broadest possible concerns about nuclear weapons. "In arms control," she says, "the most common arguments for weapons reduction are about politics or risk. For me the moral imperative has influenced most the way I think about arms control."

Georgetown his academic home. Kissinger was already affiliated with the Center for Strategic and International Studies, the think tank founded in 1962 at Georgetown by former Chief of Naval Operations Admiral Arleigh Burke and David Abshire, an adjunct professor at the university who most recently had been Reagan's ambassador to NATO. But with his appointment as an SFS professor, Kissinger began teaching a weekly two-hour seminar in American foreign policy. Though Dean Krogh recounts in his memoir that his next task after hiring Kissinger was to defend his decision to students who objected to Kissinger's prosecuting the Vietnam War, Kissinger was warmly received by those who took his class. "The criticism I get from students is that I was too soft, not that I was too tough," he told *New York Times* reporter Helen Dudar for her book, *The Attentive Eye*. "They wanted us to have won the war."

Following a hiatus during the Carter presidency, after the White House was reclaimed by the Republicans, Kissinger offered his expertise, frequently meeting with Secretary of State George Schultz. "Mr. Kissinger is widely regarded as an architect of President Reagan's recent Middle East peace proposals," said a 1982 *New York Times* article.

Meanwhile, Kirkpatrick was not comfortable at the U.N., which she once referred to as "more closely resembling a mugging than ... a political debate." She saw the U.N. as a place where member countries "blew off steam," she said, rather than looking for real solutions. That steam, she implied, was more often aimed at the United States than any other member.

Kirkpatrick was more in her element at the White House, where she sat on the National Security Council, often fiercely debating Reagan's successive secretaries of State, Al Haig and George Schultz. Reagan often favored her viewpoint, or at least enjoyed hearing it. She was such an icon of his administration's

HERSELF ALONE
Jeane Kirkpatrick was the sole woman in a group portrait of Ronald Reagan's cabinet in 1981.

> "Contrary to public opinion, we had never really been consumed with the task of 'containing' the former Soviet Union. U.S. foreign policy remained unaffected by the end of the Cold War."
>
> — JEANE KIRKPATRICK

first term that she was invited to address the 1984 Republican convention in Dallas and nominated the president for a second term, despite the fact that she was still officially a Democrat.

Kirkpatrick returned to Georgetown in 1985 and continued to write and speak on international affairs. Despite having endorsed Senator Bob Dole in the 1988 presidential primary against Vice President George H.W. Bush (whom she worried would be soft on communism), Kirkpatrick was later tapped by the younger President George W. Bush to act as a secret envoy to several Arab states in the run-up to the Iraq War.

Kirkpatrick's Cold War legacy seemed to have been cemented at the end of the 1980s, when the Berlin Wall fell, followed by the rapid retreat of communism across the former Soviet bloc. But Kirkpatrick had never thought of herself as a Cold Warrior per se. "Contrary to public opinion, we had never really been consumed with the task of 'containing' the former Soviet Union," she wrote in a book published in 2007, a year after her death at age 80. "U.S. foreign policy remained unaffected by the end of the Cold War." Though she credited Ronald Reagan

with bringing down the Soviet Union, Kirkpatrick saw European communist governments as ungainly behemoths incapable of adapting to new circumstances. They fell not because they were evil but because they were economically unsustainable.

Whatever caused the collapse, the end came almost bloodlessly and astoundingly quickly. As a junior Foreign Service officer in Poland during the Reagan years, Stephen Mull (SFS'80) was tasked with tracking the burgeoning democratic opposition. He spent so much time following dissident Poles that the Polish government eventually accused him of being an opposition ringleader and asked him to leave Poland, "never to return," he says—"or so I thought at the time." Having learned Polish prior to his assignment, he recalls thinking, "Too bad I bothered, because now I'll never go back." In fact, Mull returned to Poland as a political officer in the U.S. embassy five years later, and in 2012, he was appointed ambassador to Poland.

So rapid was the end of European communism that U.S. foreign policy took time to catch up. "By the time I retired in 1998, we hadn't really come to grips with the end of the Cold War in terms of changing policies or how we were going to function," says Michael Cotter. Even as George H.W. Bush was pronouncing a New World Order, policymakers were slow to move past the Kirkpatrick model of supporting useful dictators while transplanting American values where we could. "The expectation in the former Soviet bloc," says Cotter, who became ambassador to Turkmenistan in 1998, "was that we were going to turn them into Western democracies and instill human rights. That was not going to happen, and by the time we came to grips, it was a whole different environment."

It is possible that policymakers were preoccupied with the aftershocks of the collapse of the Communist dictatorships. In the span of three years, the two Germanys became one country,

EASTERN PROMISE
Stephen Mull and
Jack Zetkulic from
Domesday Booke 1980.

> "By the time I retired in 1998, we hadn't really come to grips with the end of the Cold War in terms of changing policies or how we were going to function."
> — MICHAEL COTTER (SFS'65)

while Czechoslovakia split in two and Yugoslavia dissolved into a patchwork of constituent states and plunged into an ethnic war. The United States' natural response was to urge the new nations to adopt the Wilsonian model of liberal democracy and self-determination as the most peaceful and economically viable way forward.

Policymakers might be forgiven for misjudging what the aftershocks of the collapse of the Communist dictatorships would mean in practice. For one thing, the change was so rapid as to defy contemplation.

For another, Eastern Europe's devolution meant rethinking the mission of some of its diplomatic institutions. USAID, a Cold War creation that had long been focused on economic development in poor countries that might fall under the sway of socialism, was now tasked with rescuing the former socialist republics of Turkmenistan, Uzbekistan, Azerbaijan, as well as Russia itself. The new directive represented a cultural shift for USAID. As Michael McFaul and James Goldgeier wrote in their book, *Power and Purpose: U.S. Policy Toward Russia After the Cold War,* "Russia's high level of urbanization, literacy, and industrialization contrasted sharply with the profile of a typical

Donald F. McHenry

IN THE EARLY HOURS OF NOVEMBER 5, 1979, IN Geneva, Donald F. McHenry (Ph.D.'63), then the United States Ambassador to the United Nations, was awakened by a call in his hotel room. The previous afternoon in Tehran, a crowd of Iranian students stormed the U.S. embassy and was holding more than 60 Americans hostage. "I was told, 'Get back to New York,'" says McHenry, who had arrived in Switzerland hours earlier for a conference on the fate of Namibia, then fighting for its independence from South Africa.

In New York, the UN quickly became the most active forum for diplomacy in the hostage crisis, in part because there were few other options. Nobody had strong lines into the new revolutionary government in Tehran.

Within a month, McHenry had shepherded Resolution 457 to unanimous approval by the Security Council, garnering the support even of the Soviet Union, which usually could be depended on to counter any U.S. measure. "Our effort in New York was to keep it an issue of diplomacy," says McHenry. "We wanted to make sure it didn't become a bilateral with the Iranians."

Nonetheless, McHenry spent the following weeks looking for some route to anyone in Iran who might have influence with the regime. "You

had to talk with anyone," McHenry recalls, "and I talked to some of the strangest people you'd ever seen in your life. Some of it was a complete waste of time. But you couldn't ignore anything."

Six months later, with Ronald Reagan's inauguration, McHenry left the UN and the State Department. In a sense, he ended his diplomatic career close to where it had begun.

As a teenager in East St. Louis, Illinois, McHenry had been dazzled by Adlai Stevenson II, who returned to the two men's home state from wartime duty as special assistant to the Secretary of the Navy. "I was smitten with this very erudite man who had gone off to DC, worked in the Navy Department during the war with very impressive people. I've often been asked how anyone coming from my small, parochial town would ever think of growing up to join the State Department. It was this illustrious character of Stevenson."

After college at Illinois State and two years of graduate work at Southern Illinois University, McHenry beat a path to Washington to fulfill the dream instilled by Stevenson. Entering Georgetown as a Ph.D. candidate in 1959, he did his course work while teaching debate at Howard University. "My interest was always in splitting my time between academia and the Foreign Service," McHenry said. "It became a race between finishing the dissertation and going into State."

State won, offering him a posting in 1963 in the Office of Dependent Area Affairs, a department of the Office of the United Nations. Conceived to support colonies in their quests for independence, "its job was to work

its way out of business," McHenry says—and Dependent Area Affairs no longer exists.

In these early years, McHenry was detailed to New York on temporary duty. It was there that he met his role model, Stevenson, who had been appointed UN ambassador by President Kennedy.

By 1966, McHenry was running the Dependent Affairs office and soon drew the attention of Secretary of State Dean Rusk, who sent him to Colombia, Peru, and Iran on special assignments. With the change of administrations in 1969, Richard Nixon's pick for State, William Rogers, called on McHenry to work with the Nixon transition team where he worked closely with Nixon's national-security team.

Even as McHenry rose at State, his proximity to decisions being made at the White House, particularly in regard to the intensifying conflict in Vietnam, convinced him to look for an exit. "I wasn't making policy, but I was close enough to it," he says. In 1970, when the United States expanded the war into Cambodia, crossing the border to attack a Vietcong retreat known as Parrot's Beak, it reignited protests against the war, bringing the resignation of several assistants to National Security Council advisor Henry Kissinger, including McHenry's friend Anthony Lake.

McHenry distanced himself by taking leave without pay from the State Department in 1971 and working out of the Brookings Institution, but after Nixon was reelected in 1973, he resigned altogether. He joined Lake at the Carnegie Endowment for the Humanities where, with Richard Holbrooke, who had left the government

AMBASSADOR
MCHENRY
*Jul. 07, 1977 -
Ambassador Donald
F. McHenry at the
UN Security Council.*

colonialism, McHenry's time was also often consumed by the negotiations for the independence of Namibia from South Africa.

When, in August of 1979, Young was discovered to have violated U.S. policy by having contacts with the Palestinian Liberation Organization and was forced out, McHenry was chosen to replace him as the permanent representative. Having inherited the position that his model, Stevenson, had once occupied, McHenry had little time for self-congratulation. Vietnam was already in the process of consolidating its February invasion of Cambodia. In November, the Iran hostage situation began. The following month, the Soviets invaded Afghanistan.

With the election of Ronald Reagan, McHenry left State again. He was inundated with offers for corporate leadership positions but chose instead to accept an offer from Peter Krogh, then dean of the School of Foreign Service, to teach at Georgetown. McHenry joined the SFS faculty in 1981 as Distinguished Professor in the Practice of Diplomacy where he taught for more than 30 years until his retirement in 2014.

"It was the ability to mix the practitioner with the theoretical," he says, as well as the opportunity to continue to practice: While at the Institute for the Study of Diplomacy, he served as special envoy to Nigeria. "The school has always accommodated that kind of thing," McHenry says. "It adds to the value of the education and the job."

Upon his retirement, the university established the Donald F. McHenry Chair in Global Human Development.

earlier, they formed a think tank within Carnegie.

For the next two years, McHenry focused again on marginal territories. He renewed his interest in Micronesia and produced a book, *Micronesia Trust Betrayed*. McHenry and Holbrooke took fellowships with the European Union and spent the summer of 1976 working in Europe on gastarbeiter (guest worker) problems.

That fall, with the election of Jimmy Carter, McHenry was called upon a second time to help with a White House transition, this time by his old friend and colleague Lake. At the end of the process, instead of leaving the White House team, he says, "I got pulled in and went off as number three at the U.S. mission to the UN," under the former Georgia congressman and aide to Martin Luther King Jr., Andrew Young.

Carter was sending a message by naming African Americans as two of his top diplomats at the UN. "Carter decided a number of things about State. One, he was not going to leave all the choice embassies to wealthy contributors, and two, he was going to appoint a number of black ambassadors."

But McHenry's long career in diplomacy, and his attention to UN affairs in particular, was intended to shore up Young, who had had little exposure to foreign affairs. So too was the presence of James F. Leonard, a seasoned arms-control negotiator, as Young's deputy. McHenry's primary responsibility was managing relations with the Security Council, which often meant checking the Soviets. "We could agree on two things," McHenry recalls. "Let's keep those other guys off the Security Council, and let's keep the budget down. Everything else was a chess match against the Soviets." As an expert in the transition from

"The last time Cotter (SFS'65) visited the area [in Vietnam], he cited the diversity in the local pig population as evidence that his tenure had perhaps opened local farmers' minds to different, more productive breeds."

THE OTHER AMERICANS
Opposite, right to left: an orphanage in Vietnam. At a livestock station in An Tho in the Mekong Delta, a U.S. advisor inspects an improved breed of pigs brought in by the U.S. Agency for International Development to upgrade the quality of the local variety. A Vietnamese farmer reads *Huong Que* (Rural Spirit) magazine, written to help farmers improve crop production. In Kien Phong province, a USAID worker inspects a thatched roof school, soon to be replaced by a new masonry school built as a self help project by local police.

AID client state in which large segments of the population lived in a village, did not read or write, and worked in the fields."

To handle this unorthodox assignment, a New Independent States Task Force was formed within USAID, drawing "the best and brightest from other divisions," according to McFaul and Goldgeier. One of those new recruits was Mark Medish (SFS'84). The son of Vadim Medish, a Russian émigré and distinguished professor of foreign studies at American University, Medish had continued his studies in government with a focus on the Soviet-era states at Harvard and Oxford after graduating from Georgetown. For good measure, he also attended law school and was clerking at the U.S. Court of Appeals in Washington when the Berlin Wall came down. "I thought, 'This is the moment to go out and do the practice of changing the world,'" Medish recalls. "I wanted to go into the government and see how I could work."

With ample connections to the incoming Clinton administration, Medish had the choice of going into the Treasury Department or joining USAID. Feeling that the critical need was for economic assistance analogous to that of the Marshall Plan, he chose the latter. He soon ended up on the new task force, acting as a liaison to the State Department's policy-planning office. "The end of the Cold War meant a shift in focus from the 'hardware' of building schools and bridges," Medish explains, "to the 'software' of transition"—institutional reform that would help the former Soviet countries move from centrally planned systems to market economies. In addition, the newly democratic states needed tutoring in the rule of law and good governance. Other transitioning countries, particularly in the Balkans, suffered breakdowns in social order and required more remedial measures—refugee relief, peacekeeping forces, and military action. Medish took part in the implementation

BROADER MISSION
In Vietnam, USAID workers like Frank Wisner, then assistant province representative, Dinh Tuong, were deployed to improve the lives of Vietnamese to secure them as allies. By 2015, Marines flew relief supplies into Nepal to assist victims of natural disaster.

Lane Kirkland

LANE KIRKLAND (SFS'48) WAS A MID-20TH-
century liberal and a staunch anti-communist, a
labor leader who unified America's trade unions
even as he endured their steep decline. A deeply
rooted Southerner, he was admired alternately for
being plainspoken and diplomatic, a philosopher
and a brute tactician. He was close to both Henry
Kissinger and Ted Kennedy. He was honored
with presidential medals by Republican and
Democratic presidents within a five-year span.

Kirkland's contradictions may have been
seeded in his education—he earned his first degree
at the United States Merchant Marine Academy
in Kings Point, New York, and served two years
aboard cargo ships in the North Atlantic during the
Second World War. In 1944, he entered the School
of Foreign Service, where he got a grounding in
history and economics as well as the profoundly
democratic convictions and international
mindset that would define his later career.

He was hired out of Georgetown by the
American Federation of Labor as a researcher
and, except for a brief period, spent the rest
of his life with the umbrella group of trade
organizations, which soon merged with the
Congress of Industrial Organizations. By 1961,
he had become an aide to the legendary AFL-

CIO president George Meany. He worked with the NAACP in convincing Lyndon Johnson to include a workplace anti-discrimination measure, Title VII, in the 1964 Civil Rights Act.

The slow ebb of union power had already begun in 1979 when Lane Kirkland took over the AFL-CIO presidency from Meany, but the election of Ronald Reagan as U.S. President the following year seemed to announce the end of unions' influence, starting with Reagan's dismissal of striking air-traffic controllers shortly after his inauguration. Kirkland fought back, convincing the United Automobile Workers, the Teamsters, and the United Mine Workers of America to return to the AFL-CIO fold over the next decade. He put the rank-and-file to work campaigning for Walter Mondale and Michael Dukakis, reestablishing the unions as a political force for the Democratic Party, even though both candidates lost their races.

Hindered, however, by 12 years of anti-union GOP rule, Kirkland found more fertile fields in foreign policy. Driven by his fierce anti-communism, Kirkland began advocating within the trade union for a group of protesting Polish shipyard workers months before they came to international attention as the Solidarity movement, raising funds from the affiliated unions, providing printing presses and radio equipment, even outfitting offices in

UNION MAN *Kirkland's diplomacy interpreted the needs of the factory floor to the C-suite.*

surrounding countries so that exiled Solidarity members could continue their work. The support would come to total more than $6 million.

He also used his leverage as a Washington insider to pressure the Reagan administration to back the dissidents. At a dinner arranged by Kissinger between Kirkland and two senior members of the Reagan White House, the former Secretary of State recalled at Kirkland's memorial at Georgetown in 1999, "the spokesmen of the 'Evil Empire' administration found themselves being castigated for not living

If Kirkland's 16 years as AFL-CIO president are remembered mostly for their difficulties, the man himself is remembered as a farsighted leader.

up to their rhetoric in the case of Poland."

After Poland's largely peaceful revolution had spread across Eastern Europe to the Soviet Union itself, Kirkland continued to see unions as a vehicle for reform in the former Eastern bloc. "Lane believed that the [Solidarity] model was exportable," according to one associate quoted in Arch Puddington's biography, *Lane Kirkland: Champion of American Labor*. Despite ample support from the AFL-CIO, however,

Kirkland's efforts to establish grassroots labor unions in the new post-Soviet states ran up against the legacy trade organizations, not to mention the problem of mass unemployment after the collapse of the Communist economies.

Meanwhile, critics at home were complaining that Kirkland was spending too much time abroad to the detriment of domestic concerns. According to *The New York Times*, as Congress was debating a crucial bill in 1993—a ban on permanent replacement workers—Mr. Kirkland was in Europe. A victory on the 1994 Family Leave Bill was seen as too little, too late. When the majority in Congress flipped to the Republicans in that year's midterm elections, it was seen as a disaster for labor. President Clinton offered to name Kirkland ambassador to Poland as an honorable way out, but he refused the post, only to be faced with a revolt from 20 union chiefs in June of 1995. He resigned two months later.

If Kirkland's 16 years as AFL-CIO president are remembered mostly for their difficulties, the man himself is remembered as a farsighted leader, one who shored up the dignity of the union cause by insisting that the issues that labor supported made life better for all Americans. It's possible to believe Kirkland's critics, and see all of his contradictions, and still admire him for the principles he stood for.

of the Dayton Accords, which would bring a slow end to the disaster in Sarajevo in the middle-1990s.

After nearly three years at State, Medish moved to Treasury as a deputy assistant secretary with responsibility for a wide portfolio covering the Middle East and South Asia in addition to Eastern Europe. He was integral to the exploits of Treasury Secretary Robert Rubin and Deputy Secretary Larry Summers in propping up the failing Russian ruble. The team, which a *Time* magazine cover story memorably dubbed "the Committee to Save the World," was "small, well-organized, dynamic, and with stellar leadership," Medish recalls.

In 2000, Medish was named senior director for Russian, Ukrainian, and Eurasian affairs on the National Security Council, where he helped set up a series of summit meetings between President Clinton and Russian President Vladimir Putin. Since leaving government in 2001, Medish has practiced law, served as vice president at the Carnegie Endowment for In-

"The end of the Cold War meant a shift in focus from the 'hardware' of building schools and bridges to the 'software' of transition— institutional reform that would help the former Soviet countries move from centrally planned systems to market economies."

— MARK MEDISH (SFS'84)

ternational Peace, and worked in public affairs and financial services. He's currently president of the Messina Group, a political-strategy consultancy. "What I didn't know when I graduated Georgetown is how well the School of Foreign Service had prepared me for the practice of international affairs," says Medish. When asked what set Georgetown apart from other foreign-affairs schools, however, Medish doesn't point to the practical instruction he got there. "The school was founded on this idea that there was theory behind the practice of international relations. That was what made it a pioneer."

Besides the chaos that followed the collapse of the Soviet Union, the end of the Cold War released other forces that had long been subsumed by the bipolar, East-West struggle. Terrorism had always existed, but it tended to be carried out by local movements clandestinely supported by major or regional powers to weaken its adversaries. Suddenly, the motivation for such state sponsorship shrunk, and terrorists and other non-state actors across Asia and Latin America turned to a host of criminal activities, primarily drug-trafficking, to replace the lost support.

The phenomenon known as narco-terrorism only increased after 9/11 brought further scrutiny to groups like Shining Path in Peru, FARC in Colombia, and most notably the Taliban in Afghanistan. Law enforcement became an increasingly significant part of foreign relations. As efforts to deprive terrorists of their illicit funding sources began to overlap, the State Department's Bureau of International Narcotics and Law Enforcement Affairs (INL), founded in 1978, took on an increasingly important role. In 2003, Deborah McCarthy, (MSFS'79), was named deputy assistant secretary for the INL.

McCarthy had come up through the Foreign Service ranks primarily as an economic counselor, with postings in Haiti, Nicaragua, and Guatemala (as well as Paris and Montreal)—ideal expe-

rience for tackling the delicate diplomacy of the drug war. The job of suppressing the drug traffic that streamed northward from Latin America in particular required a sensitive balance between the United States' overwhelming military and intelligence resources with the sovereignty and sensitivities of partner countries.

Shortly before McCarthy took the job, Peruvian military jets, acting in concert with CIA spotters over the Amazonian jungle, shot down a Cessna that turned out to be transporting not drugs but two American missionaries and their infant daughter. The young girl and her mother died in the incident,

which brought the airborne drug-interdiction efforts in Peru and Colombia to a halt for nearly two years. When those efforts resumed, under a new set of protocols negotiated by McCarthy, the program was no longer a clandestine operation, and U.S. monitors and host-nation pilots would fly in the same planes.

As the Cold War world order faded and the globe realigned, international relations came to resemble in some ways the Wilsonian period in which the School of Foreign Service was founded, when the collapse of empires had sent nations on a search for their identities and natural borders. "Nation-build-

ing and peacekeeping had become a growth industry," Ambassador James Dobbins (SFS'63) told the *Washington Diplomat* in 2017. Having served in the Clinton administration as Special Adviser for the Balkans to the President and Secretary of State during the worst of the Balkans crisis, as well as special envoy for Afghanistan and Pakistan, Kosovo, Bosnia, Haiti, and Somalia, Dobbins was an expert in nation-building. In the days after 9/11, President Bush sent him to Afghanistan and then to lead the conference in Bonn, Germany, that imposed a new government to replace the Taliban.

In 2006, Secretary of State Condoleezza Rice came to Georgetown University to outline an initiative called "transformational diplomacy." She defined it as an effort "to build and sustain democratic, well-governed states that will respond to the needs of their people and conduct themselves responsibly in the international system." While cautioning that America would be "doing things with people, not for them," she proposed that the United States "seek to use America's diplomatic power to help foreign citizens better their own lives and to build their own nations and to transform their own futures."

Jack Zetkulic (SFS'80), a Foreign Service officer, spent much of the post-Cold War period in Germany and Eastern Europe and had developed expertise in promoting democratic institutions and monitoring elections. That experience landed him a spot on the United States delegation to the talks that led to the Dayton Accords that resolved the bitter civil war in Bosnia, where he served alongside Christopher Hoh (SFS'82). Following the talks, Zetkulic became deputy chief of mission at the embassy in Belgrade.

By the time Zetkulic retired from the Foreign Service in 2008, the State Department had begun to reform around a new brand of diplomacy. The events of 9/11 had shocked the United

FULL CIRCLE
Condoleezza Rice at Georgetown during her visit in 2006, speaking about "transformational diplomacy."

> ## "Nation-building and peacekeeping had become a growth industry."
>
> — JAMES DOBBINS (SFS'63)

States out of its post-Cold War uncertainty. Suddenly, the most influential players on the world stage were not coherent states but fledgling governments trying to form nations out of disparate regions and tribes, and non-state actors like al-Qaeda. Diplomacy in Iraq and Afghanistan required its practitioners to construct nations and stabilize and empower new governments, working jointly with an American military presence.

At the time that Rice came to Georgetown, Zetkulic was director of the Foreign Service Institute, the State Department's official training academy in Arlington, Virginia. Transformational democracy, he said recently, was a turnaround for President Bush, who as a presidential candidate had said he would restrict the United States' role as a global cop and refuse to prop up failing countries. In the wake of Rice's appearance at Georgetown, Zetkulic's institute hosted a series of two-day seminars on the approach. To longtime Foreign Service hands like Zetkulic, transformational diplomacy was a return to the world in which the School of Foreign Service was founded. "It's basically a Wilsonian concept," says Zetkulic. "After World War One, the United States saw the world as a nasty place that didn't live by our values. We had to choose whether to become part of it, which we could not, or to isolate ourselves, or to transform the world. It's what we've been doing for the last hundred years."

WALSH

Father Walsh Goes to Russia

IT'S FAIR TO SAY THAT THE COLD WAR CAME earlier to the Georgetown campus than to the rest of America. Before the vast majority of American thinkers, Father Edmund Walsh had met "the Bosheviki," as he referred to Russian revolutionaries in his 1928 history, *The Fall of the Russian Empire*, and had become a committed anti-communist. By the time of his death in 1956, Walsh was far better known as an activist proponent of containing what was then accepted as the Soviets' evident desire for world domination than he was for founding a school of international diplomacy and trade.

Walsh's animus toward Soviet communism was grounded in firsthand experience. In 1922, Pope Pius XI dispatched Father Walsh to Moscow to direct the Vatican's relief efforts in the famine that had followed a severe drought, exacerbated by the Bolshevik takeover, the previous year. Walsh was also named the Vatican's representative to Vladimir Lenin's revolutionary government, which at the time had been recognized formally only by Germany.

It's not clear how Pius had become aware of Father Walsh's talents, but he had the right man. As regent of the School of Foreign Service, the Jesuit was familiar with the workings of the American government, which had mobilized the American Relief Administration to help sustain Russia through the famine. The ARA was a private organization whose effort was being overseen by Herbert Hoover, the hero of the 1914 Belgian food crisis and now Commerce Secretary under President Warren G. Harding.

Having trained in Europe, Walsh also was known to the Vatican hierarchy, as well as the upper ranks of the Jesuit order in the United States; Father Joseph Hanselman, who had been president of the Jesuits' Woodstock Seminary in Maryland while Walsh was there, had been named head of the order in America in 1918. Not least, Winifred Farrell, the sister of his close friend Father Joseph Farrell, S.J., had married Colonel William Haskell, who was running the

REACHING RUSSIA *Opposite, left to right: Joseph Ferrell, Father Walsh and William Gallagher in Moscow during Walsh's 1922-23 visit to Russia. Above, top: Father Walsh, Edward Gehrman and Joseph Feikus in the Catholic relief office. Bottom: Delivering food packages over the counter to intelligentsia of Moscow.*

ARA's operation on the ground in Russia.

Walsh's mission to Russia was the first of several he would assume on behalf of the Vatican. In 1929, the Pope asked him to join the Holy See's negotiation with Mexico's fiercely anti-clerical revolutionary government. Two years later, Walsh went to Iraq, newly liberated from British rule, to establish a Jesuit high school in Baghdad. But Walsh's time in Moscow impressed him most deeply. He would deliver some 1,400 lectures and write two of his four books on the dangers of the Soviet system.

Father Walsh left Georgetown for Russia in February of 1922, stopping in Rome to consult with Vatican officials. When he arrived in Moscow in March, Lenin was stoking the battle between the new state and the church, which was considered "counterrevolutionary." The patriarch of the Russian Orthodox Church had recently offered Lenin's Bolshevik government donations of non-consecrated gold and silver to help pay for famine relief. Lenin demanded instead all of the church's sacred vessels, and when the patriarch objected, Lenin had him arrested and eventually executed for anti-revolutionary activities.

Soon Lenin ordered houses of worship shut down, including Roman Catholic churches, and church property to be signed over to the government. In late winter of 1923, the Soviet government put Jan Cieplak, the Roman Catholic archbishop of Petrograd (now St. Petersburg), and his vicar general, Monsignor Constantine Budkiewicz, on trial

Catholics were anti-communist in theory, but no one thought it would actually become a viable political system.

in Moscow and sentenced them to death.

Father Walsh had been wary of the Bolsheviks since he'd arrived. The regime was an obstacle to his famine work, not only because of its incompetence but also in its deviousness: Covert exports of grain were leaving southern Russia even as donations of wheat from abroad were arriving in the north. "Lying is the ordinary refuge and it simply renders normal intercourse, diplomatic or commercial, almost impossible," he wrote to a superior in 1922.

Before Cieplak and Budkiewicz's show trials, however, Father Walsh hadn't regarded the Soviets as unredeemable, according to Patrick McNamara, author of *A Catholic Cold War: Edmund A. Walsh, S.J. and the Politics of American Anticommunism*. "Catholics were anti-communist in theory, but no one thought it would actually become a viable political system," he says. Even Father Walsh didn't see at first that Russia would necessarily be a problem. "If you look at his diaries, he

Communism was "the most reactionary and savage school of thought known to history."

wasn't unconvinced that you could deal with Russia," says McNamara. Though Lenin was clearly comfortable interfering with the Orthodox Church, the official position of the Bolsheviks in 1922 was no more extreme than the Jeffersonian ideal of separation of church and state. "It was the clergy trials that sent Walsh over the edge," says McNamara.

Father Walsh set to work to save the two clerics. He attended their trial and smuggled an American journalist into the courtroom to make sure the proceedings were reported on in the West. Along with diplomats from Britain, Italy, and the United States, Walsh argued successfully after their convictions to have the archbishop's sentence commuted to 10 years. (After a year in prison, Cieplak was deported to Poland and eventually died in exile in New Jersey.) Budkiewicz was executed in prison before similar pleas could be made for him.

Walsh's action on the priests' behalf angered the Russian authorities. A Soviet diplomat in Rome later railed to Vatican officials that Walsh's "American intrigues" had helped to condemn Budkiewicz. "It's Walsh that should have been executed," he said. Warned in Moscow that Walsh was an impediment to good relations, Vatican diplomats attempted to excuse Walsh's "very progressive ideas about religious liberty" as typically American. Nonetheless, by December 1923, Father Walsh was on his way home.

He didn't leave the Russian problem behind when he left the country. Walsh suggested in a scheme submitted to Cardinal Gaspari, the Vatican Secretary of State, and forwarded to the Pope, that American churches "adopt" the Catholic Churches in Russia. "Having 'nationalized' the property and declared the vessels of the altar confiscated, the Government is now instituting a system of taxation which will slowly crush the already impoverished priests and parishes," Walsh wrote in his proposal. Under his plan, the diocese of New York would be "taxed" to support the eleven St. Petersburg churches, the diocese of Boston would support the three churches of Moscow, and so on across both countries.

But Walsh came to see a threat that went beyond robbing the church of its immediate power and treasure in Russia. In his diary, he wrote that communism was "the most reactionary and savage school of thought known to history." The real evil of the Soviets was not their geopolitical ambition but their attack on the sanctity of the individual. An address in January 1945 to the 26th annual communion breakfast of the Carroll Club, a Catholic business group, at the Waldorf-Astoria

MANAGING RELIEF
Father Walsh in the mailroom of the Near East Welfare Association.

Hotel in New York captures his thinking. Father Walsh "warned that the human personality and the individual soul are being subordinated to the fascination of universal concepts, collective security, and mass production," according an account in *The New York Times*.

The threat, in other words, was not only military but one of ideas. "Being masters of propaganda themselves," he once wrote, "they have openly said the 'black international,' i.e., the Catholic Church, is the greatest enemy of the 'Red International' and to its program of de-Christianizing Russia and then the entire world." Father Walsh saw the Catholic Church and the United States, both champions of the individual as the indestructible unit of morality and politics, as communism's natural enemies.

Father Walsh was not the only voice decrying the Soviets in the Catholic Church. The Superior General of the Jesuit order for most of Walsh's life was Wlodzimierz Ledochowski, S.J., a Pole from a noble family whose antipathy toward Russia was effectively a birthright. Like Father Walsh, Ledochowski was an early opponent of Soviet communism.

But Walsh is thought to be the first American to raise the alarm about the new Russian regime. For 18 years, beginning with his return to the United States in 1924, Father Walsh gave an annual series of lectures on the dangers of communism, especially its Soviet interpretation. The series was so well attended that it had to be moved from the Smithsonian Institution to Constitution Hall, and it gained Father Walsh national attention. He was invited to address graduates of the FBI's National Police Academy, the League of Catholic Women in Boston, and the General Staff School at Fort Leavenworth, Kansas. In the audience for one of his 1928 lectures was the future president Dwight Eisenhower.

In the Washington of the 1920s, the spectacle of a Catholic priest—and a Jesuit no less—lecturing on international policy was something of a curiosity. As a political force, says Patrick McNamara, "Catholics were on the rise, but still on the margins." In the summer of 1925, thousands of members of the Ku Klux Klan, for whom Roman Catholics were still a major target, paraded down Pennsylvania Avenue. The Jesuits, as the Pope's "army," were seen as more likely than other Catholics to be seen as foreign and under papal control.

Father Walsh was able to counteract these biases with his personal connections in town. "He was a shmoozer," says his biographer McNamara. He hobnobbed with the Georgetown elite, making friends with powerful socialites such as Alice Roosevelt Longworth and Evelyn Walsh McLean. Says McNamara, "You have to understand, Walsh was a Jesuit rhetorician whose tradition was to bring people around to his point of view." At a time when Catholics were thought to be secretive and clannish, McNamara adds, "Walsh had no problem with people who weren't Catholic if they were interested in the anti-communist movement."

Other anti-communists came to rely on

Walsh's influence. The United States had broken off relations with Russia in 1918, but by the 1930s, as the Great Depression deepened, the political case for remaining aloof from the Soviets was being overwhelmed by the business case made by American executives hungry to open up the Russian market. By the time Franklin Roosevelt was elected president in 1932, the United States was the only major power that had not resumed normal relations.

The new president was intent on doing so, not only to help American corporations but because he thought Stalin could be enlisted to limit Japan's colonial expansion in China.

Father Walsh's views on dignifying the Soviet government with an embassy were already well known—the last evening of his lecture series was devoted to "The Recognition of Russia by the United States." Now he was contacted by Catholic lay leaders looking for advice on how to stop Roosevelt. He stepped up his own campaign of speeches, making his appeal on purely political grounds. In April of 1933 he appeared before representatives of a coalition of labor unions, the American Legion, and other groups opposed to the move, restricting his criticisms to the Soviets' undemocratic aims, according to the historian George Q. Flynn.

Roosevelt wasn't swayed. On October 10 of the same year, on the day he wrote to the Russian president to begin discussions that would lead to full relations, Roosevelt invited Father Walsh to the White House to explain his

SERVICE TO THE WORLD, FIRST TO LAST
Father Walsh, above, with Grigory Zinoviev in Moscow, 1923. Opposite: The Walsh Memorial Building on the Georgetown campus.

Walsh had no problem with people who weren't Catholic if they were interested in the anti-communist movement.

thinking in person. When Walsh warned that the Soviets weren't trustworthy negotiating partners, the president replied, "Leave it to me, Father, I'm a good horse dealer."

Father Walsh never abandoned the fight. In 1935, the Jesuit Superior General Ledochowski included Father Walsh in a plan to establish a new Christian social order, aimed squarely at blocking communist inroads into American life. Out of the meetings came an effort to organize schools to educate American workers on Catholic labor theory in Midwestern factory towns. He continued lecturing, speaking in all 50 states before a wide range of audiences, until 1951. He returned to writing, publishing *Total Empire: The Roots and Progress of World Communism* in 1951.

Father Walsh's books generally did well, despite the fact that his approach was more that of "an activist, not a real scholar," says McNamara. *The New York Times* called his 1928 book, *The Fall of the Russian Empire*, a "very able and trustworthy" recounting of "a

tragedy whose recital should purge the soul through pity and terror." The *New Republic* was less impressed, describing it as "stray facts floating forlornly in a riot of fiction."

Coming in the darkest days of the Cold War, *Total Empire* struck a chord. It rose to number six on the *Washington Star's* bestseller list, and number fifteen on *The New York Times's* nonfiction list. "Reviewer Mikhail Koriakov in *The New York Times*, though noting its inaccuracies, unsubstantiated generalizations, and 'unconvincing' historical parallels, nonetheless considered *Total Empire* a 'timely book,' " McNamara writes in *A Catholic Cold War*. "In January of 1952, the Catholic Writers Guild presented Walsh its award for best nonfiction book. … 'Walsh wrote as an activist attempting to persuade the public of the Soviet threat.'"

The most striking provocation in *Total Empire* is Father Walsh's endorsement of a nuclear first strike against the Soviet Union if the situation warranted such. He was writing just as the Korean War, the first global conflict of the nuclear era, had begun, and it's clear that the priest saw that war and all future engagement as determining the fate of mankind. Father Walsh's acceptance of total war reflected a widely held vision of the Soviets as "a power with no moral inhibitions." He was not alone in seeing the two superpowers locked in "a kind of cosmic poker game for the highest stakes in history."

Edmund Walsh's Cold War had become his country's in the 1950s.

01

02

03

U.S. Military Leaders

1. General (retired) John R. Allen (SSP'83), U.S. Marine Corps, Commander of International Security Assistance Force, Afghanistan, 2011–2013; **2. General (retired) George W. Casey** (SFS'70), U.S. Army, 36th Chief of Staff of U.S. Army, 2007–2011; Commanding General, Multi-National Force - Iraq, 2004–2007; **3. Major General (retired) H.D. Polumbo, Jr.** (ISD Associate 1999-'00), U.S. Air Force, Commander, Ninth Air Force, 2013–2015; **4. Major General (retired) John Fugh** (SFS'57), U.S. Army, The Judge Advocate General (JAG Corps), 1991–1993; **5. Vice Admiral (retired) William D. Sullivan** (SFS'90), U.S. Navy, U.S. Military Representative to the North Atlantic Treaty Organization (NATO) Military Committee, 2006–2009; **6. Admiral (retired) Harry B. Harris, Jr.** (SSP'94), U.S. Navy, U.S. Pacific Command, 2015–2018; **7. General (retired) James L. Jones** (SFS'66), U.S. Marine Corps, Supreme Allied Commander Europe, 2003–2006; Commandant of the Marine Corps, 1999–2003

Chapter Four

International Development and Service

T O THE DEGREE THAT MOST ORDINARY CITIZENS remember the Kosovo War at all, it is as the last in a series of complicated and bloody fights that marked the breakup of Yugoslavia in the late 1980s and 1990s. But to a generation of young internationalists, Kosovo is a touchstone. NATO, after taking little action during nearly a decade of violence in neighboring Bosnia, launched a risky bombing campaign to force Yugoslavia to accept a deal affirming Kosovo's autonomy, using its military power for the first time in a non-member state. The West's willingness to act impressed young humanitarian workers like Jeremy Konyndyk (MSFS'03), who had arrived in Kosovo in 1999 from Calvin College in Michigan as a new program director for International Aid, an American faith-based, nongovernmental organization. "Kosovo was an outlier," says Konyndyk. "We thought, 'Wow, the world will stand up for self-determination.'"

Konyndyk spent three years in Kosovo, earning praise for his cleanup efforts in the wake of the war. While earning his master's at the School of Foreign Service, he interned at the State Department's Bureau of Population, Refugees and Migration, then spent a decade at refugee-focused NGOs. He returned to government in 2013 as chief of the Office of U.S. Foreign Disaster Assistance at the U.S. Agency for International Development.

Sarah Margon (MSFS'05) didn't have the Kosovars on her agenda when she went to Eastern Europe as the war was coming to a close. Growing up in Brooklyn, she had a longstanding invitation to work for a graduate-school friend of her father's, a government minister in his home country of Sierra Leone. But when she graduated from Wesleyan University in Connecticut in 1999, she says, "Sierra Leone was engulfed in conflict. There was no way I could go." Instead, she took a sojourn to Hungary to teach English, where the Kosovo crisis came to her. "I ended up doing double duty in a refugee camp," she says. "It whetted my appetite for humanitarian work."

Today Margon is director of the Washington office of Human Rights Watch, the revered international civil-liberties advocacy group. In the nonprofit world, she has also worked on policy for George Soros's Open Society Foundation, the Center

HELPING HANDS
Opposite, German Bundeswehr helicopter lands in Prizren, Kosovo, during NATO's action to prevent genocidal violence. Right, Jeremy Konyndyk, then an office director for USAID, on the *USS Iwo Jima* in the aftermath of Hurricane Matthew in Haiti in 2016.

> "The job demanded that I meld the policy with the politics. It's the most challenging thing I've done to date."
>
> — SARAH MARGON (MSFS'05)

for National Security Studies, the Center for American Progress, and Oxfam America. Her most discernible impact on world affairs came, however, from her time as a senior foreign-policy advisor to Wisconsin Senator Russ Feingold, where she shaped the plan that became the U.S. troop surge in Iraq in 2007 and '08. "The job demanded that I meld the policy with the politics," she says. "It's the most challenging thing I've done to date."

After the fighting in Kosovo ended, NATO deployed an international force to enforce the peace deal. Among the German contingent was Gunther von Billerbeck (MSFS'05), the scion of an East Prussian noble family that had fled to West Germany after the Second World War. "My people come from a place that was but is no longer ours," he says. He had already served in Sarajevo as part of his required military service; now, with a front seat at the Kosovo crisis, he began to think of peacekeeping operations as a possible career.

Unfortunately, von Billerbeck says, "there was not much to

do in Germany with those interests." He went back to school at Heidelberg University for a master's in history and political science but chose not to pursue a Ph.D. "I found that I was interested in being a practitioner," he says. "I didn't want to read for the rest of my life." He considered joining the German foreign service, but that path too would have meant more school.

"I was at a loss," he says. "I thought about working for the United Nations, but that seemed very far-fetched. I didn't have the first idea about how to even get close to that place."

As unlikely as it seemed then, after finishing his degree at the School of Foreign Service and briefly working for the World Bank, von Billerbeck spent three years as a political affairs officer for the United Nations in the Democratic Republic of the Congo. His Africa experience in turn brought offers from strategic consulting companies, and since 2009 von Billerbeck has advised corporations investing in projects in the developing world. Today he is director of operations for the Risk Advisory

WINNING THE PEACE
Above, destruction in Peja, Kosovo, in 1999. Opposite, ethnic Albanians greet American NATO troops in the town of Gnjilane.

MADELEINE
ALBRIGHT
IS OUR MOTHER
KLINTON
GOD BLESS
AMERICA
KFOR
KFOR

Group, a business-intelligence consultancy based in London.

What these three humanitarian professionals have in common—besides Kosovo, of course—are their Georgetown degrees, which helped them shape their raw experiences on the ground into careers. When Sarah Margon arrived on campus in 2003, she felt certain she would end up at some sort of NGO, but she was unsure which sector she belonged in—health and medicine, poverty, refugees, or human rights. She sought out internships to supplement her classwork, first at the Democracy Coalition Project and then at a research institute where she studied migration patterns in Asia. (It was there that she discovered, "Nope, I'm not a researcher!")

At the same time, she took classes with Chester Crocker, a former assistant secretary of state for Africa with experience mediating conflicts in Western Sahara, Kosovo, the Philippines, and Syria. "Crocker's classes opened my mind incredibly," Margon recalls. "Conflict management was just getting under way as a discipline, and I wanted to do conflict work because of him." Margon also discovered gaps in her theoretical knowledge. "I hadn't taken international relations in college," she says. "So at Georgetown I learned the long history and the philosophy."

After graduation, Margon landed at Oxfam America, the umbrella organization for global poverty charities, then did a three-year stint at the Center for American Progress, the liberal think tank, where, as associate director of sustainable security and peacebuilding, she worked on issues relating to the whole panoply of humanitarian issues: global crises, human rights, foreign aid, and good governance—all of which came into play again when Senator Feingold asked her to help him think through the redeployment of U.S. troops from Iraq. The care and thoughtfulness that was needed to figure out what would fill the vacuum drew upon every bit of her preparation.

CAREER IN CARING
Opposite, Sarah Margon in eastern Chad with Oxfam America. This page: Margon on a panel in Washington, DC, discussing the Rohingya crisis and a camp on a beach in the Greek islands set up by refugees who refused to stay at overcrowded and dangerous detention centers.

Carol Lancaster

ROBERT GALLUCCI, WHO KNEW CAROL Lancaster (SFS'64) for more than three decades and preceded her as dean of the School of Foreign Service, remembers offering his old friend a ride to a conference they were attending at Swarthmore College in Pennsylvania one midwinter weekend. There was a catch: He was planning on driving his convertible Honda S200, and no matter the weather, he'd have the car's top down. Lancaster, to Gallucci's surprise, accepted.

The last thing to expect from Carol Lancaster was the expected. Partly this was due to her tremendous energy and her willingness to put herself in unaccustomed situations. It was also a practical necessity for a woman who was determined not to allow her gender to stop her from going where women had not previously gone. She was one of 30 females in her class at Georgetown's School of Foreign Service, which had only begun admitting women in 1953. Lancaster traveled to South America and the Middle East while still in her twenties. She later became the first woman to serve as deputy administrator of the United States Agency for International Development.

Doing the unexpected was Lancaster's method of breaking down barriers. It is perfectly in keeping with Lancaster's personal and career arc that she was the first person in her family to attend college, only to become, a half-century later, the first woman dean of the school that she attended.

Lancaster grew up in Maryland, only miles from the Georgetown campus, and graduated from Oxon Hill High School, but the sense of a larger world was already impressed upon her by the time she finished school. It was the beginning of a time "when the Vietnam War and civil rights divided parents from children and fed many demonstrations in downtown Washington and fights over the dinner table," she later wrote. "It was a time of political activism and anger."

In her senior year she was awarded a Fulbright fellowship and went to Bolivia, a culture shock for her baffled parents, who had expected her to come back to Maryland and look for a job, as well as for Lancaster: The poverty of 1960s South America opened her eyes to the fact that economic development was needed before any political or cultural change could occur.

At the London School of Economics, where she earned her doctorate, she met Mehdi Ali, an Iraqi who became her first husband—and her first Arabic teacher; eventually Lancaster would master six foreign languages in all. It was then that she became fascinated by the Middle East and Africa.

She returned to Washington in 1972, breaking into government work as a federal budget examiner before joining the staff first of Rep. David Obey of Wisconsin and then Richard C. Clark of Iowa. In 1977 she moved to the policy-planning staff at State and three years later became deputy assistant secretary of state for Africa.

Africa became her chief concern—and the topic of five of her 10 books. It was in Africa that she saw that women's lot in developing countries was not just a matter of gender equality but

MAKING STRIDES
*Above, Lancaster,
President DeGioia and
Costa Rica President
Laura Chinchilla
Miranda (G '89) in
2011 Commencement
Exercises.*

foreign aid spending in the decades to come," she wrote in *Foreign Affairs* in the fall of 2000.

But Lancaster saw that if USAID was to focus on humanitarian aid, not politics or economic development—a concern she wanted to see devolved to the World Bank— it needed to keep its autonomy from the State Department. As deputy administrator during the Clinton administration, Lancaster often raised this warning with the First Lady. Afterward, she used the press as a bully pulpit and appeared before Congress to argue that the priorities of diplomats and of development workers were very different.

"The danger is that the more USAID is drawn into the State Department orbit," she told a Senate subcommittee on international development in 2009, "the more its development assistance programs and the more all U.S. aid programs become tools primarily of diplomacy."

In the meantime, Lancaster took on more administrative roles on campus, directing the School's Master of Science in Foreign Service program and heading up the Mortara Center for International Studies. In 2010 she was named dean of the School of Foreign Service.

In the three years that she held the post, Lancaster helped found the Georgetown Institute for Women, Peace and Security and a new SFS master's degree in Global Human Development.

In late 2013, Lancaster was diagnosed with a brain tumor and took a leave of absence from Georgetown. In April 2014, she stepped down. Lancaster died October 22, 2014, at the age of 72.

key to those countries' advancement. "She understood the pivotal role that women played in development, not just in history but also as agents of change," Melanne Verveer, former chief of staff to First Lady Hillary Clinton, told the *Washington Post* in 2014. Verveer and Lancaster got to know one another on trips with the First Lady to the developing world.

Lancaster came back to Georgetown in 1981 as a professor of politics and taught for a dozen years before being tapped by USAID administrator Brian Atwood to be his deputy. Though she spent only three years at the agency before returning to the School of Foreign Service, her experience at USAID defined much of her later thinking and writing,

and for the rest of her life she was considered one of Washington's foremost advocates for the reform of foreign-aid practices.

As the Cold War ended, Lancaster, once again a professor at Georgetown, began pushing for foreign aid to be the instrument of "a U.S. diplomacy of values," directed more at humanitarian goals than short-term political ones. She wanted to see money spent to expand human rights and quality of life. She believed aid could soften the blow of globalization by funding training in poor countries that would allow them to better exploit globalized trade and investment. "Support for development and democracy abroad will not disappear, but they will not be among the major priorities for

Margon also led a 2010 effort to require the Obama White House to work out a strategy to deal with the Lord's Resistance Army, the militant cult around "prophet" and warlord Joseph Kony that had been terrorizing Uganda and South Sudan.

Margon credits Feingold for his willingness to allow her to "play hardball with the executive branch"—a necessary temerity she learned at Georgetown. "So much of my work has been pushing back against institutions," she says. (No less, she adds, in defending human rights in the age of Trump.) At the School of Foreign Service, "nobody was soft and squishy. I often recall what my professor Princeton Lyman once told me: 'Get to the table and have something good to say.'"

Like Margon, Jeremy Konyndyk ended his time in Kosovo unsure about what kind of humanitarian work he wanted to do. "Is this the course I want to stay on?" he recalls asking himself. "I wanted to be exposed to other tracks."

For that exposure, Konyndyk turned to Georgetown. In his classes, and especially during his internship at the State Department's refugee bureau, Konyndyk learned "how the United States thinks about policy decisions." After three years executing in the field, his tenure at State also gave him the perspective

of an aid donor. "Over the course of my career, I've been able to see the dynamic between headquarters and the field," says Konyndyk, who went on to serve as a country director for several other NGOs before returning to government. "Things work better in the field if you can understand why distant bureaucrats are making the decisions they are," he says.

In the years since the Kosovo crisis, the NGO world has experienced a boom. Fueled largely by an increase in private-sector funding, the NGO sector has ballooned to a trillion-dollar-a-year "industry." Governments contribute just 8 percent of the assistance going to undeveloped countries, down from some 70 percent less than two decades ago. The remaining 90 percent comes from the private sector. "As wealthy, northern, western governments scale back on public spending, the void is being picked up by the NGO sector," says Stéphane Dujarric (SFS'88), spokesperson for the Secretary-General of the United Nations. "A portion of the One Percent is stepping up and spending huge amounts of money, and the growth of their mega-NGOs, like the Gates and Rockefeller foundations, is creating an alternative ecosystem."

As it has grown, the world of humanitarian assistance has become globalized and interconnected. The smallest NGOs have found it easier to merge their missions with behemoths like Gates, Ford, and Rockefeller, or with governments and multilateral bodies like USAID and the World Bank.

So powerful are the large NGOs today that the United Nations has come to depend on them to implement their programs. "There is a growing understanding at the UN that, in order to achieve our sustainable agenda, we need to open our doors to NGOs," Dujarric says. "It's a fight for visibility and relevance."

At the same time, nonprofits have become ever more intertwined with the business of developing markets. When Gunther von Billerbeck decided to leave Africa in favor of for-profit consult-

> "… I've been able to see the dynamic between headquarters and the field. Things work better in the field if you can understand why distant bureaucrats are making the decisions they are."
>
> — JEREMY KONYNDYK (MSFS'03)

ing in England (in large part because his classmate, and now wife, Sara Kanafani, had enrolled in a Ph.D. program at Oxford), he saw his move less as a departure from humanitarian work than simply taking another avenue. "I wanted to do something where I stayed connected to peacekeeping and conflict- and crisis-management, but I determined I could do that for different kinds of organizations in difficult markets. I got exposure not only to foreign affairs but also to commercial interests, and how those two connect."

No one has melded these two strands of economic development, perhaps, as much as Stephen Cashin (SFS'79). Cashin was born in Libya in 1961 while his father, Richard Cashin, was an official for the Point Four program, a precursor to the United States Agency for International Development. He grew up in Ghana and Indonesia as his family followed his father to postings around the world.

The vast preponderance of funding in that postwar period came from the United States, the United Kingdom, and other Western governments. Their goals were largely political—the point of building infrastructure and making agricultural improvements in those days was to bring developing nations into the United States's sphere or keep them from straying into the Soviets'. "The separate study of how to manage economic-development programs, how to finance them, and the role that bilateral donors and international agencies could play in promoting and accelerating the process was really a postwar phenomenon," Richard Cashin said in a 1993 interview. He was among the pioneers.

The dollars were judiciously spent—less than $5 million was enough to grab the attention of the Ethiopians in the early 1960s. Today, Africa is the second-largest mission field (after Southeast Asia) for NGOs; its funding would be counted in the top 10 economies if all of its countries were one sovereign nation. But Africa is also a thriving mission field for the World Bank, the Overseas Pri-

vate Investment Corporation (OPIC)—the United States government's development lending agency—and free-market investors. In this mix, the lines between purely humanitarian work, quasi-governmental funding, and capital investment are becoming blurred.

"My intent was always to work in the development space," says Stephen Cashin, who returned to the continent as a Peace Corps volunteer in Tanzania after graduating from Georgetown. But a bad experience in his next job, with a philanthropy in Kenya, soured him on NGOs, and Cashin returned to the United States to get his MBA. His familiarity with Africa attracted HBSC, the Hong Kong-based bank, which hired him in 1984 to open a branch of its subsidiary Equator Bank in Kenya. In 1998, he left the bank to found the Modern Africa Growth and Investment Company for

DEVELOPING STORY
Born in Libya to a federal aid worker and his wife, Stephen Cashin has spent his career in Africa, beginning in the Peace Corp in the 1980s, opposite. He remained focused on Africa throughout his career.

George Tenet

IF, AS IS SOMETIMES SAID, GEORGE TENET (SFS'76) was an "accidental" Director of Central Intelligence, few other directors have been as well qualified, changed the agency as much, or headed it during such a difficult time.

In 1996, President Clinton tried to replace the retiring DCI, John Deutch, with his National Security Advisor, Anthony Lake. But Senate Republicans stalled Lake's nomination, citing Lake's political baggage connected to the Clinton campaign-finance operation, and Lake withdrew. Clinton offered them Tenet, who was deputy director at the CIA.

Though Tenet had come from the National Security Council and considered Lake a mentor, he was also a former Senate Intelligence Committee staffer who had maintained good relations on the Hill. The Republicans made Tenet, at 44, the second-youngest director in the agency's 50-year history.

Unlike the standoffish Deutch, Tenet walked the halls and ate in the employee cafeteria at the CIA's headquarters in Langley, Virginia, often joining mid-level analysts for impromptu lunches. His democratic style was a balm for agency veterans who had seen four directors in a little more than five years.

Tenet's comfort in the director's seat came in part from his long preparation for the post. The son of Greek immigrants—refugees from the turmoil in their homeland and the Balkans in the wake of the Second World War—Tenet grew up in Queens listening to his parents discuss the geopolitics that had disrupted their lives and those of their relatives. "My father was a keen student of history, politics, and the world," Tenet recalls. His father's trek to the United States included a stint as a coal miner in France, during which he had come to lionize Charles de Gaulle; among Tenet's earliest memories is his father cheering the French war hero and president as he rode up Fifth Avenue in an open car.

Tenet began college at a branch of New York's state-university system in the Bronx, but "I knew I had to get to Washington," he says. "I grew up with this palpable sense of the Second World War and a violent civil war in Greece, and it captivated me. You're a kid in Queens and you have those aspirations, and what do you know? I

thought, 'This is the place—I've got to get here.'"

Already imbued with a sense of public service, Tenet found in the Jesuits at Georgetown the ideal of duty to "something bigger than you and bigger than your professional interests."

He encountered the same sensibility in U.S. Senator John Heinz of Pennsylvania, who hired Tenet—now boasting a master's from Columbia as well as his Georgetown degree—as a legislative assistant in 1983. "The toughest guy I ever worked for," Tenet remembers, Heinz "taught that it was a privilege to be in public service, and therefore you had to work harder than anyone else. You had to know your stuff. God help you if he knew more than you did about an issue."

After two years, the senator, who had an interest in arms control, sent Tenet to the Senate Intelligence Committee just as the Reagan White House was negotiating the Intermediate-Range Nuclear Force Treaty. Tenet helped draft the committee's report on the ability of the American intelligence community to monitor the agreement, and was named staff director of the comittee at the age of 35.

As a result, four years later Tenet was one of the most knowledgeable Democrats about intelligence when Bill Clinton took over the White House. He was asked to help the transition team with intelligence matters, and then to stay on and work for National Security Advisor Anthony Lake. After two years at the White House, Clinton named Tenet as Deutch's deputy director at the Central Intelligence Agency.

"I've been really lucky," Tenet says, "in the sense that I always worked for really good

Right: Tenet watches President Bush's televised address on 9/11. Opposite: in the Oval Office as the invasion of Afghanistan began.

people who took an interest in my career and cared about the development of young people."

In 1996, Tenet was made part of the American delegation sent to restart a peace process. "We understood that the security cooperation between Palestinians and the Israelis had to be built from the ground up," Tenet says. "The security and the peace negotiation were interlinked."

The Middle East would take up the lion's share of Tenet's time in the Clinton administration. He often served as interlocutor between the Palestinians and Israelis, "trying to move them in a direction of cooperating with each other." At the Wye River Conference in 1998, the security agreement Tenet and the security team negotiated provided the foundation to keep the political talks going forward.

In July of 1997 he was given the top job at the CIA. Seven years into the post-Cold War era, the "peace dividend" had taken a toll on budgets, effectiveness, and morale. More than a quarter of the CIA's foreign stations had been shut down. "The FBI had more people in New York than we had case officers in the entire world," Tenet recalls.

Slowly, Tenet began putting the CIA on a growth track. "Not having money forced us to

think about what really mattered. It was analysis, clandestine operations, and technology." Under Tenet's leadership, recruiting and applications increased, the agency's training facility was rebuilt, and its curriculum changed. To ensure that the CIA was able to compete in cyber-intelligence, says Tenet, "we built a venture-capital firm that today is second only to Google Ventures in the number of deals done every year."

In the middle of this comeback for the agency, as Tenet was having breakfast with his old intelligence committee boss, Sen. David Boren, in Washington, planes flew into the World Trade Center towers and into the Pentagon.

The strikes began a run of difficult years in the public eye for the CIA, for Tenet, and for the intelligence community as a whole. Critics wanted to know how the Al Qaeda threat had been missed or discounted. In the wars that followed, the CIA's reputation suffered, even as it helped to fight two insurgencies abroad and stymie further foreign attacks on U.S. soil. Tenet was personally blamed for inaccurate intelligence that furthered the White House's case for going to war with Iraq.

"Anytime anything goes wrong in a democracy," Tenet says today, "and this went wrong,

there are consequences. This is something we will live with the rest of our lives. Certainty is something you should challenge your entire life."

Meanwhile, he was responding to the crisis. Four days after the 9/11 attacks, he presented President Bush with a war plan for Afghanistan. Two weeks later, CIA operatives were on the ground, working with local sources to craft a counterinsurgency operation. "It's probably one of the most remarkable stories in the history of the organization," he says.

The CIA's resilience showed too in its pursuit of nuclear disarmament. For almost a decade, a small group of agents, working with British intelligence, had been tracking the exploits of A.Q. Khan, Pakistan's senior nuclear scientist, as he exported know-how and technology to North Korea, Iran, and other rogue states. In early 2004, the CIA finally had enough evidence to confront the Pakistani government. "I was able to look President Musharraf in the eye and show him stolen centrifuge documents that had been provided to the Iranians," says Tenet.

The demise of Khan's network sent a warning to other countries that the CIA was still a potent adversary. "All that played into Libya being disarmed without a shot being fired," says Tenet.

For Tenet, the intelligence business has been as satisfying as it has been unexpected.

"If you asked me, do I have any regrets?—not a single regret," he says. "It played out in the most interesting way."

Before 9/11, says Tenet, "the FBI had more people in New York than we had case officers in the entire world."

OPIC. Eight years later he created Pan-African Capital Group, an investment fund that backs banks, insurance companies, and other financial infrastructure in sub-Saharan Africa. Since 2014, he has been the chairman of Africare, one of the oldest philanthropies.

David Weiss (MSFS'78) also began life as the son of a foreign-service officer. Weiss grew up moving between Washington and his parents' postings in Yugoslavia, India, Germany, and Switzerland. As a young teenager in New Delhi in the mid-1960s, he was exposed to the wonders of the Green Revolution and watched as Peace Corps volunteers flooded the country. After studying government at Hamilton College, he came to Georgetown for his master's in 1976 hoping to get into development. "At the time I graduated, I was thinking about USAID, the World Bank, or the UN Development Program. But it occurred to me that if I went into the Foreign Service on the economic side, it would be the best of both worlds."

Weiss chose to go to Haiti as the U.S. embassy's economic officer in Port-au-Prince. His interest in the undeveloped world recommended him to the director of the Peace Corps, where he served as special assistant to the director for two years, followed by two years as an assistant to Deputy Assistant Secretary of State John Whitehead, a former Goldman Sachs co-chair who would later make nonprofit leadership a focus of his philanthropy.

As the emphasis in development moved to the private sector, Weiss's interests moved to trade. "Trade was playing a bigger role," he says, noting that multinational corporations had come to see undeveloped countries as emerging markets. "In one sense, international development is developing capacity, but there is ever more focus on developing capacity for trade—regulations, tariff schedules, bureaucratic capacity." In 1987, Weiss moved to the Office of the United States Trade Representative, where he stayed for a decade, working on NAFTA and other major trade deals, until he was hired by the law firm DLA Piper, where he advised clients on trade matters.

In the early 2000s, a friend from his Peace Corps tenure told him about Global Communities, an NGO that works at the local level to improve trade and sustainable development. "I became enamored of the organization," Weiss says, "and in 2004 I was invited to join the board. I soon saw the writing on the wall." In 2010, he was named President and CEO of Global Communities.

The combination of business-minded donors, leaders like Weiss and Cashin, and the sheer volume of dollars involved in humanitarian work has resulted in a rise in professionalism in NGOs. Private-sector donors have higher expectations of a measurable return on investment and greater accountability. Some veteran aid workers are troubled by the trend, worrying that a field once populated with passionate altruists has been taken over by data-driven technocrats. Konyndyk sees his younger self as an example of the older model. "I was a warm body willing to

GLOBAL REACH
Global Communities President and CEO David Weiss inspects a construction site after the 2010 earthquake in Haiti and meets with beneficiaries of a Global Communities project in northern Jordan.

go to a tough place—I just wanted to help," he says, adding: "You can't really get jobs on that basis anymore. There's much more of a premium today on having a skill set. And that's a good thing."

The NGO boom has also greatly expanded opportunities for working for good. "There are so many options for someone with a natural enthusiasm for humanitarian work now," says Mark Yarnell (MSFS'09). "You can get your overseas experience sitting at a desk in Nairobi writing grants, or intern at home office and get your experience that way. There is still the Peace Corps, where you can get out into a rural area and learn about yourself, and there are these NGOs with budgets of millions of dollars."

Like Konyndyk, von Billerbeck, and Margon, Yarnell stresses the importance of pragmatic training combined with real-world experience to produce professionals who are capable of being both effective and empathetic.

It was a chance meeting with von Billerbeck in the fall of 2006 that led to Yarnell's Georgetown degree. Two years before, Yarnell had been so intent on working in Africa that he'd flown to Kinshasa without a job and knocked on doors until he found one. While working for a small British philanthropy implementing USAID projects in Congo—or, as Yarnell puts it, "figuring out how to get cement from A to B" —he was having a beer at a rooftop bar one evening when he fell into conversation with a German who turned out to be the UN's local political director.

Yarnell told von Billerbeck that he liked the hands-on work and the opportunity he had to get off the beaten track into remote areas. "But I didn't feel suited to the logistics," he says. "I was so much more interested in the broader policy side. I wanted to know how decisions made in DC or at the UN affected what happened in the field."

Von Billerbeck told Yarnell about his time at Georgetown, explaining that he too had wanted to avoid academics for their own sake. "I was interested to hear that most of the professors were practitioners," says Yarnell. "I wanted those practical skills to be more employable." When he began his MSFS coursework the following autumn, he vowed to himself that he'd be back in the field within three years.

Yarnell successfully avoided academia, but he never made it back to Africa in a development role. After graduating from SFS in 2009, he took a two-year Henry Stimson Center fellowship on Capitol Hill, working on aid policy with Senator Richard Lugar, a former chair of the Senate Foreign Relations Committee. Since leaving the Stimson Center, he has been working for the nonprofit Refugees International, where he helps develop policy and frequently visits stricken areas in the Middle East and Asia to see how policy impacts refugee response on the ground.

Given the flood of funding into nonprofits, and the numbers of new recruits, the skill most urgently needed for today's NGOs may be business administration. "NGOs often suffer from poor management," says an executive at an NGO headquartered near Washington, DC. "Those people whom we make managers

> "You can get your overseas experience sitting at a desk in Nairobi, or intern at home office. ... There is still the Peace Corps, where you can get out into a rural area and learn about yourself, and there are these NGOs with budgets of millions of dollars."
>
> — MARK YARNELL (MSFS'09)

Mick Mulvaney

SWEPT INTO CONGRESS WITH THE 2010 TEA party Mick Mulvaney (SFS'89) spent much of his time in the House agitating against government spending and opposing regulation, which led by the swamp-draining logic of the Trump administration to his appointment as the White House budget chief and chair of the Consumer Financial Protection Bureau. His insurgent approach to these jobs soon resulted in Mulvaney's being named acting White House chief of staff in January 2019. The transplanted (from North Carolina) South Carolinian is every bit as much an accidental politician as his boss. Mulvaney was the first Republican to be elected from South Carolina's 5th District since Reconstruction, beating a Democrat who chaired the House Budget Committee and who had for 28 years dismissed his opponents as unfortunate formalities. He'd secured permission from his wife to run for the seat by assuring her that he'd never win.

Born in Alexandria, while his developer father worked for the National Association of Homebuilders, Mulvaney was raised in Charlotte.

A Krogh Scholar at the School of Foreign Service who formed his habit of daily Mass while at Georgetown, Mulvaney had little idea what he wanted to do next. Given a full scholarship, he attended law school at the University of North Carolina and went on to Harvard Business School, graduating with no more notion of his future than when he had left Georgetown. He worked for his father then on real-estate projects of his own, which led him to follow local politics.

One day a neighbor he didn't like called to ask for his support in running for the state legislature. "My reaction to hearing he was running was, 'Really? So am I.'" Two years later he was a state senator, and two years after that he went to Washington, espousing a libertarian-leaning, "leave-me-the-hell-alone" brand of conservatism.

But he didn't like Congress as much as he'd expected. Instead of the robust debates and policy discussions he was used to in South Carolina, the U.S. House was "a fundraising gig," he says. "You were expected to yield your voting card to someone further up the food chain and then go out and raise money for the party."

The Tea Party's accomplishments, which include bringing down Speaker of the House John Boehner, were largely in what they refused to do, Mulvaney says. "If anything, I take credit for stuff I didn't vote for, because the bills did get better. We did bend the spending curve down temporarily." The conservative wing of the Republican Party, he says, also made

improvements in how the House is run. "Boehner would have been a great speaker in 1950. We started to change how the House is managed."

Serving on committees on finance, economic growth and small business, Mulvaney was an advocate of smaller government, lower spending and curtailed services, attitudes that went a long way to earn him the OMB post. Preparing the federal budget and administering government funds, it turned out, was the policy-heavy job Mulvaney wanted in the first place—"what I thought I was going to come to Congress to do," he says.

For the first time in his career, he put his macroeconomics degree to work. "I didn't use my education in a professional sense until I got to Congress," Mulvaney says. "Now, what I learned in my 20s, I'm using in my 50s." At the Office of Management and Budget, he kept his School of Foreign Service macroeconomics textbook under his desk; he says he frequently consulted the 30-year-old primer on international payments and trade.

Mulvaney was sometimes frustrated in his attempts to introduce "small c" conservative principles into the massive federal budget. "It's already hard to change the culture of an entity this big," Mulvaney admitted in an interview in his massive, Gilded Age office in the Old Executive Office Building shortly before moving to his White House role.

As President Trump's acting chief of staff, Mulvaney now has more ways to exercise his impact. By his own admission, that impact does not include taming the president. A policy wonk and a veteran of the Hill — experience his two predecessors in the job lacked — Mulvaney can afford to be ambitious in the role. And while some in Washington may be surprised to see a Tea Partier rise so quickly to his key government post, Mulvaney apparently knows what he wants to get done. Reportedly, it is the one job in the administration this accidental politician wanted badly enough to lobby the president for it.

Preparing the federal budget and administering government funds, it turned out, was the policy-heavy job Mulvaney wanted in the first place — "what I thought I was going to come to Congress to do."

often have no training in management. They have been promoted because they have served and excelled in the field."

That too may be changing with the latest generation to enter the development field, whose members are as liable to wear business suits as to be decked out in khaki. After graduating with a concentration in international development, Anthony Gao (SFS'11) chose not to take the accustomed path of other students, many of whom go straight to the World Bank or an NGO. Gao elected instead to go to work for the management consultancy McKinsey & Company. After two years at McKinsey, he took a leave to join the Gates Foundation in his native China.

A tide of economists and statisticians is sweeping into humanitarian work as well, responding to the new push to measure the cost-effectiveness of aid programs and to maintain accountability. Captivated by her economics classes at the School of Foreign Service, Eliza Keller (SFS'09) went on to get a master's in public administration at Columbia University. Much of her work since has focused on the effects of data-crunching on foreign assistance—positive and negative. In a 2015 journal article, Keller cautioned: "Ignorance of the fallibility of data could soon become a missed opportunity for the development community to truly capture the realities of how people in poor countries live, work, and make decisions."

Today Keller is a policy manager at the Abdul Latif Jameel Poverty Action Lab, a research center at the Massachusetts Institute of Technology that uses scientific methods to test the effectiveness of poverty programs.

At Georgetown, economic principles are not necessarily removed from humanitarian principles. Darcy Olsen (SFS'93) credits her economics classes at Georgetown with informing her innate sense of social justice.

Raised in modest circumstances by a single mother in Utah,

> ## "In seventh grade I made a petition to stop the clubbing of seals and walked it around the trailer park where we lived and sent it off to Greenpeace. It's like asking an artist, 'When did you begin loving art?'"
>
> — DARCY OLSEN (SFS'93)

Olsen says she developed her own sense of justice as a girl. As a third-grader, she wrote to Ronald Reagan suggesting a few ideas about how to improve the lot of the homeless. "In seventh grade I made up a petition to stop the clubbing of seals and walked it around the trailer park where we lived and sent it off to Greenpeace," she says. This empathy, she believes, is inborn. "It's like asking an artist, 'When did you begin loving art?' " When she came to campus, she decided to live in a dormitory hall reserved for students who were interested in community service, even though she spent little time in any formal service organization.

Living in Utah after graduation, she heard from her classmate Gene Healy (SFS'93), who was working at the Cato Institute, the libertarian think tank back in Washington. Olsen went to work as an editor at Cato's *Regulation* magazine, soon stepped up to become a junior analyst, and before long opened a new policy department on child welfare.

In 2001, Olsen returned to the West to take over as CEO of the Goldwater Institute, a think tank named for the conservative U.S. senator and former presidential candidate Barry Goldwater and based in his home state of Arizona. There she learned quickly about managing a nonprofit. "I discovered we were a million dollars in the red," she says. Olsen had to root out the accounting errors that had allowed the nonprofit to mismanage its funds,

HELP FOR THE YOUNGEST
Olsen's advocacy for children through her nonprofit Gen J grew out of her own experience as a foster parent.

then put the organization on a path to solvency. "I reformed it so that it worked like a private-sector business," she says.

Cognizant that an advocacy group could not afford to sit still while it restructured, Olsen also set about refocusing the group's policy positions. "If your purpose is to create change, you have to keep changing yourself," she says. "We just kept adding new pieces." Olsen hired an investigative journalist to look into the operation of government agencies. She established a litigation arm, led by now-Arizona Supreme Court Justice Clint Bolick, to fight for its causes in court. Today the Goldwater Institute is among the most highly rated political advocacy organizations by Charity Navigator, the nonprofit watchdog group.

Olsen's Goldwater Institute has also made headlines. Focusing on local issues that have national reach, it has challenged public subsidies for the Phoenix Coyotes hockey franchise and bolstered Arizona's property-protection laws to reduce eminent-domain takings. Working at the state level, Olsen says, allowed Goldwater wider latitude to effect policy changes that might be blocked if it were fighting at the national level. "The idea was to do a lot of model work on the state level in Arizona," says Olsen, "then let other states adopt what we'd done." The institute's greatest success has been "right to try" legislation that allows terminally ill patients access to drugs and other therapies that show promise but have not been fully approved by the Food and Drug Administration. Though controversial, the concept has become popular, and Goldwater's legislation has formed the template for right-to-try laws in 38 states.

In 2017, Olsen left the Goldwater Institute to found Generation Justice, dedicated to reforming foster care for children taken from their parents. "When I learned about economics, I became someone who believes in economic freedom," she says. "That was the big change that came at Georgetown."

INFLUENCERS

Denis McDonough

HISTORY LIKELY WILL REMEMBER DENIS McDonough (MSFS'96) for a walk. In August of 2013, Syrian dictator Bashar al-Assad had dropped sarin gas on a rebel stronghold near Damascus, killing more than a thousand people and crossing a "red line" that President Obama had said would result in Western military action.

As Washington awaited the president's "Go," Obama summoned Denis McDonough, his chief of staff and a voice of caution, and went for a walk with him on the White House's South Lawn. Forty-five minutes later, the two returned to announce that Obama would seek congressional approval for a military strike, which never came.

It made perfect sense that McDonough would be the final counsel to Obama on a decision so difficult that it would be debated for the rest of Obama's term in office.

McDonough, whose master's thesis at Georgetown was on the long, violent civil war in Ireland known as the Troubles, seemed to enjoy peeling away the layers of complicated issues. McDonough was the last and longest serving of Obama's five chiefs of staff, exerting a quiet but profound influence on a president whose wariness of power was reflected in his constant questioning of his advisors.

There was nothing fated, however, about McDonough's entry into Obama's inner circle. A Catholic from the Minneapolis suburb of Stillwater, McDonough received his MSFS degree and was hired as an aide to the House Foreign Affairs committee with responsibility for Latin America. Three years later he became a foreign-policy advisor to a fellow upper-Midwesterner (and Catholic), U.S. Senator Tom Daschle of North Dakota, and helped write the Iraq War resolution in 2003. After Daschle lost his seat in the 2004 election, McDonough joined the staff of Senator Ken Salazar, a freshman lawmaker from Colorado, as legislative director.

It was Mark Lippert, another former Daschle hand, who recruited McDonough to join Obama's presidential campaign in 2007. Lippert, a Navy reservist, was serving as top foreign-policy advisor to the first-term senator from Illinois when he was called to active duty in Iraq. He tapped McDonough to replace himself.

As the campaign grew, McDonough eventually headed a staff of more than 300 policy advisers; he moved into the West Wing with the president in January 2008, assigned to the National Security Council, serving first as head of strategic communication and then as

STRATEGIC LISTENER
President Obama and Denis McDonough in the Oval Office in 2009.

its chief of staff. Eighteen months later, he was named deputy national security advisor.

It was in this role that McDonough appeared to become Obama's foreign-policy fixer, parachuting into the effort to aid Haiti after a catastrophic earthquake in January 2010 and over the next three years attending to nearly every major effort, from the troop withdrawal in Iraq to the Benghazi attack to developing the policy known as "Afghan Good Enough" that resized U.S. involvement in Afghanistan and led to the handover of security to Afghan forces.

"When it comes to national security, Mr. Obama's inner circle is so tight it largely consists of Mr. McDonough," *The New York Times* commented in 2010.

Still, it was a bit of a surprise when Obama asked McDonough to be White House Chief of Staff at the beginning of his second term. The

---

On national security, "Mr. Obama's inner circle is so tight it largely consists of Mr. McDonough," *The New York Times* once said.

---

president still seemed focused primarily on domestic policy, which McDonough had rarely touched. Obama made clear that his choice was guided by McDonough's skills as a motivator and attention to detail. "Were it not for him, we wouldn't be as effective a White House," the president said in announcing his appointment.

As chief of staff, the former Hill aide grasped that neither domestic nor foreign policy could go well without Congress, whose members, Republicans and Democrats alike, suddenly felt heard—not least because the new chief of staff wasn't above giving them his home number. His relationships paid off during the rocky rollout of the Affordable Care Act and the White House's inability to avoid a shutdown in late 2013, both of which McDonough managed by listening to criticism from any quarter. Meanwhile, his expertise on foreign matters, from the opening of relations with Cuba to the forging of the Iran nuclear-arms deal, made him indispensable.

It was during this crunch time of Obama's second term that McDonough became the translator of the president's mind, ever-present, getting things done while strictly obeying Obama's "no drama" dictum. "He really seems to be an extension of the president," then-House minority leader Nancy Pelosi told *Politico* magazine in the waning days of the Obama administration.

Since the end of the Obama administration, McDonough has kept a characteristically low profile. He thinks, writes, and speaks about issues he encountered as White House chief of staff, from refugees to American education, and has taken a position as senior principal with the Markle Foundation, a philanthropy dedicated to using technology to improve lives. McDonough's brief is to help American workers learn how to meet the needs of the digital economy.

Members of Congress

1. **Harry Sandager** (SFS'21), Representative from Rhode Island, 1939–1941; 2. **Harrison Williams, Jr.** (attended SFS'41), Representative from New Jersey, 1953–1957, Senator from New Jersey, 1959–1982; 3. **James Kee** (attended SFS), Representative from West Virginia, 1965–1973; 4. **Robert Bauman** (SFS'59, L'64), Representative from Maryland, 1973–1981; 5. **Philip Sharp** (SFS'64, Ph.D.'74), Representative from Indiana, 1975–1995; 6. **Richard J. Durbin** (SFS'66, L'69), Representative from Illinois, 1983–1997, Senator from Illinois, 1997–present; 7. **Bill Schuette** (SFS'76), Representative from Michigan, 1985–1991; 8. **Henry Cuellar** (SFS'78), Representative from Texas, 2005–present; 9. **Luis Fortuño** (SFS'82), Resident Commissioner from Puerto Rico, 2005–2009; 10. **Glenn Nye** (SFS'96), Representative from Virginia, 2009–2011; 11. **Mick Mulvaney** (SFS'89), Representative from South Carolina, 2011-2017; 12. **Debbie Dingell** (SFS'75, S'98), Representative from Michigan, 2015–present; 13. **Stacey Plaskett** (SFS'88), Delegate from the Virgin Islands, 2015–present; 14. **Dan Sullivan,** (MSFS'93, L'93), Senator from Alaska, 2015–present; 15. **Mike Gallagher** (SSP'12, MA'13, Ph.D.'15), Representative from Wisconsin, 2017–present; 16. **Stephanie Murphy** (MSFS'04), Representative from Florida, 2017–present; 17. **Xochitl Torres Small** (SFS'07), Representative from New Mexico, 2019–present; 18. **Lori Trahan** (SFS'95), Representative from Massachusetts, 2019–present

SFS in the Private Sector

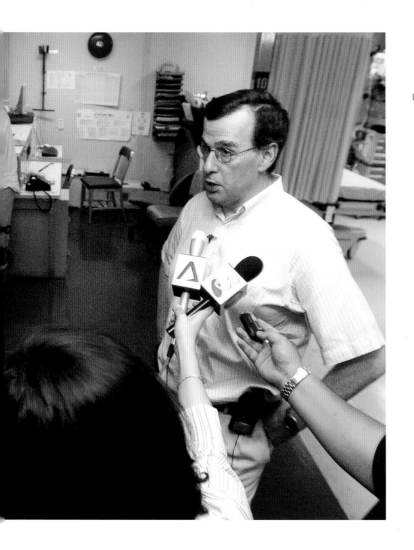

T

HIS HISTORY BEGAN WITH JOHN MAYNARD KEYNES'S Londoner, sitting in his bed ordering the world's goods to his doorstep. Today, that Londoner needn't even pick up the telephone; with one click, he can buy any one of a wealth of items while conferring by Skype with his spouse, who might be traveling for her job in Korea or China. Globalization has come to define the early 21st century as much as it did in Keynes's time a century ago, when the School of Foreign Service was founded and the prosperous American consumer in New York or Chicago was about to replace Keynes's Londoner as the most powerful consumer of international business.

If at its outset the School of Foreign Service's primary role in the expansion of global commerce was sending highly qualified Commerce Department consuls and vice-consuls to far-flung ports, today it prepares its graduates to take part in commerce directly. Over the past century, graduates of the school have made their marks in banking, telecommunications, manufacturing, marketing, medicine, transportation, and, not least by raw numbers or by impact, as lawyers who facilitate and finalize the agreements that make these industries thrive.

Yet even as the scope of the school's education has vastly expanded, its mission has remained essentially the same. "There is value and purpose in understanding the world," says Frank Lavin (SFS'79), a former Undersecretary of Commerce and U.S. ambassador to the Republic of Singapore un-

UNDERSTANDING ASIA
In 2006, Frank Lavin, then U.S. ambassador to Singapore, aboard the *USS Mercy*, as it takes on supplies for the relief of tsunami victims in Indonesia.

"In 1919, we suddenly had the largest economy in the world, and for the first time we sent guys out to Japan or Thailand and told them, 'Figure out what's what.'"

— FRANK LAVIN (SFS'79)

der George W. Bush. And as central as the School of Foreign Service has been to diplomacy and government, most of its students apply the understanding they have gained in its classrooms to business. "This is where the world was in 1919," Lavin says. "Foreign policy, which only erupted in times of crisis, was not as central. In 1919, we suddenly had the largest economy in the world, and for the first time we sent guys out to Japan or Thailand and told them, 'Figure out what's what.' "

A hundred years later, this service is still necessary. As tightly integrated as our world is today, businesses still require interpreters of other commercial cultures. Executives still need to know how to tell which locals are the best businesspeople, how to form partnerships with them, and how to avoid the wrong kind. They need to know which of their products translate into markets abroad and need to learn the mechanics of buying and selling in unfamiliar places. But "soft" barriers, Lavin says—the difficulties of finding a warehouse, hiring local employees, or doing the paperwork to incorporate locally—are more likely to defeat a business trying to gain a foothold in what is already a mystifyingly difficult market to crack.

In 2010, Lavin founded Export Now, a web startup that helps companies gain entry into China's booming e-commerce market—and which exploits all of Lavin's government and pri-

vate-sector experience. A Phillips Andover graduate from Canton, Ohio, Lavin felt unchallenged in his first year at Georgetown. He approached his academic adviser to ask what was the hardest course available to undergraduates. That turned out to be a class in Mandarin, which, given China's persistent isolation from the rest of the world, had virtually no practical use for an American college student at the time. "It was like taking Latin," says Lavin. After getting a master's degree at Johns Hopkins SAIS, he returned to Georgetown for a master's in Chinese language and history. In 1981, he joined Ronald Reagan's White House, first on the National Security Council staff and eventually as the President's director of political affairs. He moved to Commerce under President George H.W. Bush as an Asia hand, and when Bill Clinton won the presidency, he left the government for a job in banking. His return to government, and to Asian affairs, came when he was named ambassador to Singapore after the Republicans retook the White House in 2001. In George W. Bush's second term, Lavin was made Undersecretary of Commerce, and afterward took a job with Edelman as chairman of the public-affairs giant's Asian Pacific Rim business. "It's a very specialized set of skills," says Lavin.

As new markets open up and government regulation becomes more complex, these kinds of skills have become increasingly valuable. Since the early 1980s, especially, a number of advisory firms have sprung up to guide companies through thickets of policy and politics, domestic and international.

They have come to employ the former diplomats, legislators, and policymakers who earlier would typically find "of counsel" perches at Washington's prestigious law offices. At McLarty Associates, a strategic advisory firm, Jorge Guajardo (SFS'93), Mexico's former ambassador to China, offers expertise on Latin America and the Far East. Boston Consulting Group employs

DEVELOPING EXPERTISE
Mike Simakovsky (MSFS '05) shaking Leon Panetta's hand.

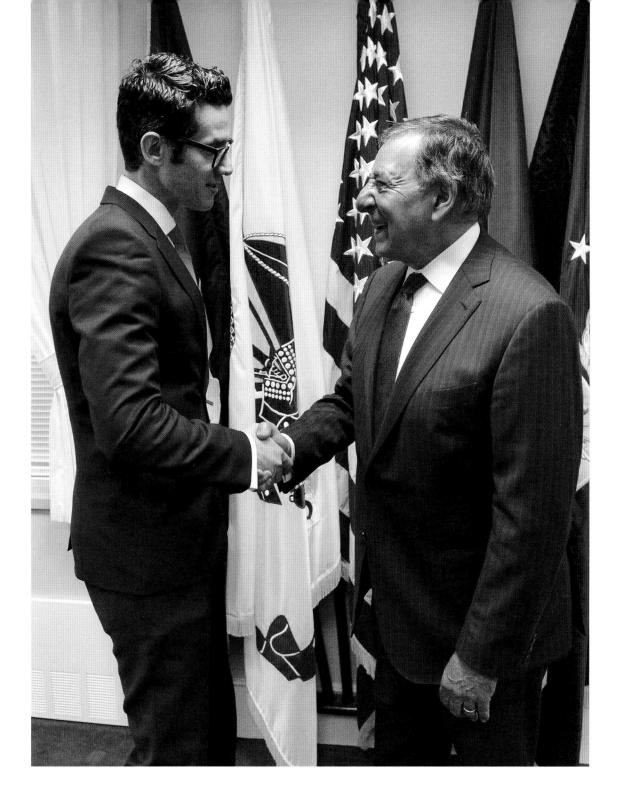

Bailey Hand (MSFS'03), who, shortly after earning her master's degree joined the Defense Department. After working briefly with Iraq's transitional government in the aftermath of the American invasion, she shifted to Afghanistan and spent nearly a decade shuttling from the battleground to Washington, representing the needs of deployed U.S. personnel on Capitol Hill and the concerns of ordinary Afghans at the Pentagon. In 2013, she left her job as Defense Secretary Leon Panetta's special assistant and went to the Boston Consulting Group, where, she says, she solves problems for global corporate clients in much the same way that she did for the Department of Defense.

Mark Simakovsky (MSFS'05) was a Fulbright scholar in the former Soviet republic of Georgia after earning his master's at the School of Foreign Service, pursuing his interest in Russia during a period of relative quiet in Moscow. "In my generation there was an interregnum when people didn't understand why I was focusing on Russia," he says. "They thought I should become a generalist or concentrate on other areas, like India or Pakistan."

But Simakovsky, the son of immigrants from the Soviet Union and grandson of a Red Army officer, continued to develop his expertise, which led to a job at the Pentagon working for the Under Secretary of Defense for Policy, Eric Edelman, under Defense Secretary Robert Gates. When the White House changed hands in 2016, he left to join Beacon Global Strategies, a security-oriented advisory group founded by former Panetta chief of staff (and Georgetown University grad) Jeremy Bash (C'93). "The customer is different," he says, "but the type of stuff I deal with is similar."

These careers, however, are more exemplary than representative; the great majority of School of Foreign Service graduates have gone into business or law, and, rather than reflecting the emphasis on international affairs, the work they pursued often followed broader trends in the economy. "Most of us became

Dick Durbin

WHEN DICK DURBIN (SFS'66) LEFT HIS WORKING-class hometown of East St. Louis, Illinois, in the late summer of 1963 to attend Georgetown—flying to Washington in an airplane for the first time in his life—few of his neighbors had heard of the university, much less of the exotic-sounding School of Foreign Service.

It was exactly the lure of the unknown that attracted Durbin when he came across a catalog in the Pius XII Library at St. Louis University, where he was enduring an unhappy freshman year as a commuter student. "I wanted an education adventure," the U.S. senator from Illinois says today. "I had no idea that I was preparing myself for this job."

The transition to the School of Foreign Service was difficult for Durbin, who struggled to catch up with classmates who'd already had a year to become accustomed to the school. As a transfer student, he wasn't given a room in the dorms, so he took an apartment with a couple of other transfers off Calvert Street, north of campus. In Professor Carroll Quigley's two-semester course on the development of civilizations, he met students who were taking it for the third time after failing it twice. "Quigley scared the hell out of me," Durbin recalls.

But the rising junior, who went back to East St. Louis at the end of that year, was no longer a sheltered Midwesterner. He had attended a soirée at the Ecuadorean embassy at the invitation of the ambassador's daughter, his classmate Margarita Correa. And he had stood vigil in front of the White House in the hours after President Kennedy's assassination. "I was living in the place that made the front page of the newspaper every day."

It wasn't until his senior year that Durbin found the path that would make this consequential place his own. After hearing his Calvert Street roommate John Stucker (SFS '66) talk about his Senate internship, Durbin applied to join the office of legendary Illinois Senator Paul Douglas, a liberal economist and Chicago politician who had served in the Senate since 1949. "They gave me a chance," says Durbin, and he acquitted himself well enough that in the summer following his graduation, Douglas asked Durbin to work on his re-election campaign. Durbin gave up his summer job in a slaughterhouse to work for Douglas. By the time the senator lost that fall, the victim of his advancing age and a stance on Vietnam that was out of sync with the times, his young recruit had gone back to Georgetown to begin law school. But Durbin's time on the campaign trail in Illinois had left him "head over heels" for electoral politics.

It had also introduced him to politicians up and down his home state. His J.D. in hand, Durbin was

---

His consistency is rooted in his faithfulness to the principles of his Midwestern mentors.

EARLY START
*Now the senior U.S.
senator from Illinois,
Durbin first worked
on the Hill while
a transfer student
at Georgetown.*

hired as legal counsel to Illinois Lieutenant
Governor Paul Simon, who would go on to the
U.S. Senate in 1984. After unsuccessful runs
for state senator and lieutenant governor,
Durbin was elected in 1982 to represent
Illinois's 20th District in the House of
Representatives, Abraham Lincoln's former seat.

In 1996, he moved into Simon's Senate seat
with his predecessor's strong endorsement;
two years later he was invited to join the
Senate leadership as Assistant Majority
Whip. After the 2004 midterm election, he
rose to be the Democratic Whip. A liberal
stalwart, Durbin receives high marks from
unions, environmental advocates, and pro-
choice activists (despite his opposition to
abortion early in his career), and a consistent
"F" from the National Rifle Association.

His consistency is rooted in his
faithfulness to the principles of his Midwestern
mentors: "My political views were formed
by Douglas and Simon," says Durbin. Yet
he is the first to acknowledge that leaving
Illinois for Georgetown was his first big step
toward making a career of those values.

lawyers," recalls Conrad Everhard Jr. (SFS'82) of his classmates, citing the billable-hours revolution that, beginning in the 1960s, caused law firms to bulk up with thousands of young associates to take advantage of the new profit model.

Everhard, whose attendance at Georgetown was "preordained" by the high esteem in which his father, an alum and a refugee from World War II, held the school. Yet despite an upbringing abroad that made a Foreign Service career a "logical" choice, Everhard says he was lured by the high stakes of aggressive corporate takeovers and the opportunities promised by big law.

The lure of adventure mixed with serious money has drawn some School of Foreign Service graduates into finance. One of the most influential financiers in recent American history was the late Michael Mortara (SFS'71), who, with his wife, Virginia, helped found the Mortara Center for International Studies, housed in the Mortara Building just off campus at 36th and N streets, Northwest. Matching his Georgetown degree with an MBA from the University of Chicago, Mortara joined Salomon Brothers, the legendary investment bank, in 1974. There, working with his mentor, Lew Ranieri, Mortara was instrumental in developing the market for mortgage-backed securities, a business that became a cornerstone of Salomon Brothers' outsized profits of the time, according to the *Financial Times*. Mortara became an indelible character of Wall Street's go-go 1980s era when he appeared in Michael Lewis's chronicle of the time, *Liar's Poker*. In 1987, Mortara moved to Goldman Sachs, where he made the mortgage-securities department into one of the investment bank's profit centers. He had taken over GS Ventures, a Goldman e-commerce subsidiary, when he died at age 50 of a brain aneurysm.

Besides lawyers and financiers, the School of Foreign Service has turned out entrepreneurs, hoteliers, architects, newspaper

INNER CIRCLE
Opposite: Mark Simakovsky, center left, at a meeting with defense secretary Robert Gates. This page: Jeremy Bash with Gates' successor, Leon Panetta, center.

and magazine reporters and editors, and software programmers. Graduates have gone into health care and utilities, popcorn and plastics. Many joined family concerns, from shoe shops to law offices. Aristides Nickles (SFS'38) went home to Middletown, New York, to work in, and eventually take over, his family's restaurant, the Coney Island Café, and ran it for many years afterward.

Examine the business careers of School of Foreign Service graduates over the past century and you see an undeniable pattern of international involvement. Samuel C. Bartlett, Jr. (SFS'20) was not atypical of his class. The eldest son of missionaries from a prominent New England family, Bartlett was born in Kyoto, Japan, and began his education in Massachusetts before transferring to Georgetown. In January of 1920, he sailed from San Francisco to Tokyo with a team of architects and engineers from the newly formed George A. Fuller Construction Company, a subsidiary of New York's dynastic Starrett real-estate firm. As Jeffrey W. Cody describes in his book *Exporting American Architecture 1870–2000*, the Fuller company had been invited by Japanese government officials to build modern office buildings in Tokyo for the Nippon Oil Company and the Mail Steamship Company as symbols of the country's newfound commercial might—"monuments of steel, concrete and granite dedicated to the god of business and trade," according to the *Far Eastern Review* at the time. Bartlett, fluent in Japanese, was hired as a traffic manager and translator.

Bartlett would remain in Japan, later working as a branch manager for the General Sills Importing Company in Yokohama and Kobe, for the rest of the 1920s. After the Great Depression struck, he returned to Massachusetts to attend law school but was sent back overseas by the Navy for the duration of the Second World War. His knowledge of Japanese made him valuable as an intelligence asset; he was sent to Australia

DYNASTIC AMBITION
Aristides Nickles from
1938 *Domesday Booke.*

"Besides lawyers and financiers, the School of Foreign Service has turned out entrepreneurs, hoteliers, architects, newspaper reporters and editors, and software programmers. Graduates have gone into utilities, popcorn, and plastics."

and put in charge of interrogating prisoners of war. At the end of the conflict, he joined General Douglas MacArthur's staff at the surrender conference in Manila and later at war-crimes trials. After his military service, for which he won the Legion of Merit, Bartlett returned to Massachusetts and his career as a lawyer for the commonwealth. He passed away in 1966.

The list of those who gravitated toward foreign postings in corporate jobs is long. The Second World War and the Korean conflict seemed to redouble graduates' taste for working abroad. John Fitzpatrick (SFS'41) came to Georgetown from his Irish-born father's avocado and lime orchards in California and upon graduation was commissioned into the wartime Navy. When the war ended, Fitzpatrick stayed in the service, serving 18 years and retiring in 1959. He promptly went to work for

Gulf Oil, spending the next two decades overseas.

Others managed to have international careers while staying home. Sven Langmack (SFS'40) was a Washington, DC, native whose international influence came from his parents, Ida Hansen, a Danish gymnast, and a fellow Danish athlete, Holger Christian Langmack. After meeting at the 1912 Olympics in Stockholm, the couple moved to the United States, where Holger Langmack became a well-known conditioning coach for, among others, Knute Rockne. By the late 1950s the family had settled in Washington, and Sven's parents found employment as physical-education teachers at DC public schools.

In 1936, Sven Langmack was awarded a scholarship to Georgetown. After graduation, says his son J. Christian Langmack, he took a job with a manufacturer of farm implements in the Cleveland

Cheryl Long

IN THE LATE 1960S, MARGARET HARRISON, then the registrar at the School of Foreign Service, received an application from Cheryl Long (SFS'71), a senior at Washington, DC's Coolidge High School and an African American. There had been African American men on campus since the 1950s but no African Americans among the women who had begun to attend in 1954.

A Southerner raised by a single mother, Harrison "had known her own tribulations and was very alert to racial considerations," says Long. When the registrar encountered her application, Long says, Harrison went in to see Father Joseph Sebes, then dean of the school. "She put my app in front of him," says Long, "and said, 'It's time.' "

It was gender, however, more than her race that proved the greater influence on Long's future.

When Long appeared for her interview with Father Sebes, she was accompanied by her father, Reverend C.M. Long, then pastor of Mount Airy Baptist Church in Washington. "In those days," says Long, "nice young ladies didn't come to a meeting with an unknown man alone." Her father, who had grown up in

a heavily German-American neighborhood in East Orange, New Jersey, noted the dean's European accent and began the conversation by asking, "Sprechen Sie Deutsche?" Long soon found herself a spectator to the discussion about whether she would attend Georgetown.

Once admitted, Long was told that she would not be allowed to live on campus: Women were few on campus, and female dormitories were fewer. Women with homes in the Washington area weren't given living quarters, so Long, who wanted the full college experience, ended up at Syracuse for her freshman year. Harrison persisted and lured her back with the offer of a room.

Four years later, Long became the first African American woman to graduate from the School of Foreign Service.

But as graduation approached, Long, who had been working toward a Foreign Service appointment since middle school, saw that only a very few of her female classmates were being taken by the State Department. "It had never crossed my mind that I wouldn't get into the Foreign Service because of my gender," says Long, but there was no mistaking the pattern. At last, not one but two of her professors, Lev Dobriansky and William O'Brien, separately pulled her aside. "Look," they told her, "this isn't going to happen. You need to go to law school."

She entered Georgetown Law in the fall of 1971 and while there impressed her professors sufficiently to be nominated upon graduation for a clerkship with Spottswood Robinson III, then a judge on the U.S. Court of Appeals for

the District of Columbia (which he would later head as chief judge). A graduate of Howard Law School and later a dean there, Robinson is best known today as one of the lawyers working for the NAACP's Legal Defense and Education Fund in the early 1950s who filed the case that would become *Brown v. Board of Education*.

But to the DC legal community, Robinson was primarily known for his thoroughness and elegant writing, skills he passed on to his clerks. "That got me in the door as a federal prosecutor," says Long, who during seven years as an assistant U.S. attorney worked extensively with the DC Metro Police and the FBI, sometimes getting convictions other prosecutors had given up on. "I ask a lot of questions," she says. "That is how I learn."

Long then moved to the Department of Justice's Division of Land and Natural Resources, trying corporations that violated federal environmental laws and, on the civil side, enforcing the Superfund and Clean Water Acts.

Her decade of experience defending the federal government and prosecuting federal offenders gave her an instinctive sense of how government agencies work—and how they ought to. In 1985, the Public Defender Service for the District of Columbia asked Long to re-engineer an agency that suffered from insufficient planning and desultory management.

LIFE OF INQUIRY *As a prosecutor, administrator and judge, says Long, her success has come because "I ask a lot of questions. That's how I learn."*

"The personnel rules were just two pages long," she says. She was the first African American woman to direct any major city's public-defender office, reshaping it into a modern department. A year later, she was also appointed to the Committee on Grievances, which investigates ethical misconduct of attorneys practicing in the United States District Court for the District of Columbia.

In 1971, the year Long graduated from Georgetown, the Nixon administration had

Though she was the first African American woman to graduate from SFS, it was gender, more than race, that determined the course of her career.

reorganized the District's court system, which since the beginning of the republic had handled both federal cases and local suits, as the courts of any state would. Under the Nixon plan, part of the dispensation that granted home rule for the District, DC got its own Superior Court and a Court of Appeals, though for years judicial nominations tended to go to those favored by members of Congress.

As a nearly lifelong DC citizen, and with her supremely balanced legal resume, Long aimed for an opening on the Superior Court bench. "I

pulled together people who would help me out," Long says, "Democrat and Republican." To make its final choice, the White House consulted Joseph DeGenova, then U.S. attorney for the District of Columbia, who recommended Long. She was sworn in in May of 1988.

During her time on the Superior Court, Long, who still serves as a senior judge, has heard civil, criminal, and domestic cases and presided over the probate and tax divisions, writing opinions on nearly every kind of judicial decision.

The crucial turn in Long's professional life—her pursuit of a legal career—may have taken place at Georgetown, but she feels that she arrived on campus more than prepared to become a pioneer for women and African Americans. Indeed, she remembers the campus even during the turmoil of the late '60s and early '70s as "a sedate place," with few African American students to agitate or coalesce around a minority consciousness. "There were more Iranian students than black students," she recalls. "We were exotic. It just wasn't an issue."

Instead, she says, "I took my cue on how to operate from my parents," who had always encouraged her to do whatever she felt she could and pushed her to go where her difference didn't matter. Says Long: "I was never in a situation when there were not kids of different kinds around me."

TERMS OF SURRENDER
The end of the war with Japan and the ensuing occupation gave American business an entree into the reconstruction of Japan's infrastrucure.

area, where he married and made his home in then-rural Gates Mill, Ohio. When he returned from military service at Fort Knox after World War II, the overseas market for agricultural tools was booming as Europeans got back on their feet.

With his School of Foreign Service training and his growing expertise in international business, Langmack soon became a major proponent of exporting for Ohio manufacturers. When President Dwight Eisenhower ordered the creation of a nationwide network of state export councils, Langmack served on Ohio's council, as well as on the Northern Ohio Export Council and the Cleveland World Trade Association. As Ohio's industrial power faded in the second half of the 20th century, Langmack's efforts were credited with helping sustain the Cleveland area's economy, in part by convening conferences on

exporting for local business people. Not long before his death in 2003, the *Christian Science Monitor* portrayed Langmack as "divid[ing] his time between overseeing his industrial washing systems company"—a business he bought and ran with his sons—"and 'finding local companies that are good candidates to export, and teaching them how to do it.'"

Given Georgetown's location in the nation's capital and its faculty's firsthand familiarity with the workings of government, the international flavor of these careers is hardly surprising. But many of those who graduated in the postwar years seem to have been motivated as much by a call to public service as by a taste for life abroad. Even among those who followed their SFS degrees with law school often landed in the Justice Department or other government agencies. Philip

"When we arrived, Georgetown had been influenced
by the influx of veterans. It was very professionalized. Within a couple
of years after we graduated, things were so different."

— PHILIP VERVEER (SFS'66)

Verveer (SFS'66) had come to Georgetown from the suburbs of Chicago with the idea that he might go into the Foreign Service. Once on campus, he became active in school affairs, running for class president his junior year and working to broaden the horizons of what had become, in the wake of Father Walsh's death, a somewhat depleted and insular School of Foreign Service. With several other students, Verveer organized the Conference on the Atlantic Community (CONTAC), a gathering of university professors from as far away as Russia, to talk about issues confronting the world.

At the same time, Verveer became interested in the civil-rights conflicts brewing in the United States and used his student-government position to organize bus trips for students to assist in the Southern civil-rights crusades. Verveer took the Foreign Service exam and as a senior was invited to apply, but he opted instead for law school at the University of Chicago. He joined the Justice Department in 1969 with hopes of being assigned to the civil-rights division.

Instead Verveer found himself in the antitrust division—civil rights was no place for a young husband and father, he was told, as it required too much travel. There the idealistic young lawyer took up a complaint from a fledgling telecommunications company called Microwave Communications Inc.—MCI—against AT&T, then the country's phone company. Wielding its monopoly power granted by the Federal Communications Commission, AT&T was inhibiting MCI's ability to offer long-distance microwave phone service by linking up to AT&T's network. In 1973, Verveer suggested that Justice begin an investigation. Soon, the 31-year-old lawyer was leading the case, arguing that AT&T needed to be dissolved.

Though the suit would ultimately be successful, resulting in the creation of the "Baby Bells," Verveer left the case in 1977

CHANGING GUARD
Opposite: '60s student government, with Philip Verveer kneeling, right, and Bill Clinton standing second from left. Verveer and his wife, Melanne, at a military ball. This page: Verveer at a civil rights rally.

Edward Garlich

WHILE IT IS NOW CUSTOMARY FOR HEDGE funds and others who trade stocks to track legislation and other goings-on in Washington that might affect their business, it wasn't until 1974 that Edward V. Garlich, Jr. (SFS'68) figured out a way to make a commodity of that information.

Garlich had come to Washington as an aide to Senator Gordon Allott, from Garlich's hometown of Pueblo, Colorado, with the understanding that one day he'd run for office himself. He won admission to the School of Foreign Service, and began attending while continuing to work for Allott. He remembers the early 1960s as a difficult time for the School of Foreign Service. "A lot of faculty had left and we had lost a bit of credibility," he recalls. In Washington, however, he caught view of a larger world. After five years of service to Allott, he says, "I walked in and said, 'This is not for me.' I wanted to have more impact."

Graduating in 1968—his Senate duties had caused him to take six years to get his degree—Garlich was hired as an economist for the trucking and rubber industries, focusing on international trade, and became a lobbyist for the American Gas Associations, working the Senate side of the Hill. Not long after Richard Nixon was re-elected president, he was drafted by the administration to work on domestic policy. Before he could start, however, Garlich realized that the information he was providing to his corporate bosses could be equally interesting to stock traders, especially those with the largest portfolios who could make big money on small shifts in trade policy or defense appropriations. "Our concept was we could sell strategic research to institutional investors," he says.

Garlich assembled a group of partners, including Sterling Green, a former business reporter for the Associated Press. He contacted lawyer friends who had clients who were institutional investors in San Francisco and London. His first obstacle was convincing his prospective customers why they needed to know what he could provide. "In 1973, you had to tell people why Washington was important." The oil crisis that year was a boon for the business. "I made my reputation on the oil and energy business."

The problem was how to get paid for this new kind of intelligence. "I had to find people with a trading desk," Garlich recalls, who could compensate the Washington Research Group for the trades made using its information. He initially formed an alliance with the investment bank Drexel Burnham Lambert, until the bank folded in the 1980s. Since then, Washington Research Group has had nine different owners, always retaining Garlich as the head of the business, until his retirement in 2013. That year, the magazine *Absolute Return + Alpha*, which tracks the hedge fund industry, cited Washington Research Group as a top analyst in its field.

That field has grown in the years since the Washington Research Group was founded to include competitors such as the ISI Group, the Potomac Research Group, Washington Analysis—in addition to the in-house political information units maintained today by major banks. Interpreting Washington to business, to the world and even to itself has become an industry of its own.

In 1973, Garlich had to tutor institutional investors in San Francisco and London and New York on why Washington was important. Then came the oil crisis. "I made my reputation on the oil and energy business," he says.

"I found that I had become a
communications lawyer.
I fell into a part of the economy
that was growing like crazy."

— PHILIP VERVEER (SFS'66)

after failing to convince his superiors at Justice to devote more resources to it. "It didn't require clairvoyance to see that it would take 25 to 30 lawyers," he says, not to mention an extensive discovery process with access to all of AT&T's internal correspondence. "There was an odd failure of imagination," says Verveer.

Leaving what came to be recognized as the business case of the century "turned out to be a blessing," says Verveer. "I shouldn't have been in charge of that case—I was too young, for one thing." He moved to the Federal Trade Commission's Bureau of Competition, which led to his hiring as chief of the cable bureau at the FCC at a time when the same issue was animating the AT&T case at Justice—how to incorporate outside technological innovation into a monopoly's static grip on the country's communication system. Even as it was trying to deny use of its lines and switches to MCI, AT&T was champing to take advantage of the new flow of digital information going out over its wires. "It became important to divide the two things," says Verveer. "The Bell system had an incentive to want communications regulation to extend to IBM and the other entities trying to use transmission systems to move data." For the sake of restraining AT&T's monopoly power while allowing innovation to bloom along its networks, the FCC had to find a way to draw a line between the telephone business and

the entities that were making use of its services.

The decisions Verveer made at the FCC laid the groundwork for regulation and fair use of the internet today. "To the extent that I can claim having made any lasting contribution to society," he says, "it was there." Availing himself of ideas about deregulation that had begun to come out of universities and his own education in law and economics—"and having read a lot of AT&T internal mail," he adds—"I had a pretty good notion of what was going on." In 1980, Verveer was instrumental in putting out an FCC pronouncement known as Computer Inquiry II. The decision established that dominant firms like AT&T should be more firmly regulated than fringe companies (or what we call startups), and it drew a sharp line between basic services—those that purely transmit information—and advanced services—transmissions that do something, whether that's paying a bill, turning off your air conditioning while you're out, or simply searching for a web bargain. "We think about AT&T being regulated and Google not," says Verveer. Freed from regulation and AT&T's hegemony, new modes of communication could flourish.

Shortly afterward, Verveer left government for private practice. "I found I'd become a telecommunications lawyer," he says. "I fell into a part of the economy that was growing like crazy." For the next three decades he worked on cellular licensing and satellite matters, the growth of cable television, and the formation of internet standards from three Washington law firms. By the turn of the new century, regulating telecommunications had become an international priority. In 2009, President Obama appointed Verveer to the position of U.S. Coordinator of International Communications and Information Strategy, an ambassadorial post that came with a Deputy Assistant Secretary of State title. This last, international turn in Verveer's government service (he returned to

OLD FRIENDS
Verveer with his
college friend and
President, Bill Clinton.

Paul Clement

ASK EVEN A CASUAL OBSERVER OF THE
Supreme Court how to describe the cases
Paul Clement (SFS'88) has argued there and
you're likely to hear the words "consequential"
and, particularly since the former U.S. Solicitor
General left government in 2008, "conservative."
He has argued to repeal the Affordable Care
Act on behalf of 26 states and to preserve the
Defense of Marriage Act at the behest of House
Speaker John Boehner. He handled a high-
profile immigration suit for the state of Arizona, a
voter-registration case for South Carolina, and a
North Carolina electoral-districting fight. Another
description would be "frequent." In his seven
years as Solicitor General and Principal Deputy
Solicitor General for the George W. Bush White
House, Clement argued 49 cases before the High
Court. Since returning to private practice, Clement
has appeared there at least eight more times,
more than any other lawyer in the 21st century.

Those who have followed Clement's career
more closely point out that his High Court
cases don't conform to any type. Clement has
represented California state-prison inmates
in their suit to relieve overcrowding, Dr. Dre's
recording label, and the National Football League
in the fallout from the Deflategate scandal.

If his selection of cases contains some
surprises, few are likely to think of America's
foremost constitutional litigator as an expert in
international law. And yet: "The irony is that in
going to Georgetown, I was acting on an interest
in international things," says Clement, who as a
debater in high school became fascinated with
the Soviet Union and the moral and legal issues
its behavior raised. "Not the diplomatic corps,
but initially I thought that an international legal
practice would be a great fit." Clement points
out that some of the most significant cases he
argued for the Bush White House concerned
the war on terror and provisions of the Geneva
Convention, most famously *Hamdi v. Rumsfeld*,
which questioned whether American citizens
could be treated as enemy combatants.

"I ended up doing a fair amount of international

———

**Even I've been surprised to see
how many international issues
I've ended up dealing with.**

law in the Solicitor General's office," he says.
In private practice, he adds, "Even I've been
surprised to see how many international issues
I've ended up dealing with," including, in 2017, the
Supreme Court's consideration of whether foreign
nationals may use United States courts to sue a
corporation under the 1798 Alien Torts Statute.

The consensus seems to be that no matter
what the topic of concern is, Clement is a master
at reading his audience of nine and tailoring
his arguments to what their questions reveal
about their leanings in the case at hand. Known
for his complete immersion in the details of his
appeal, Clement works without notes, freeing
him to respond in the moment to the particular
points the justices are raising. The spectacle
of Clement's almost collegial parrying of their
doubts has been described by *The Washington
Post* as watching "speed chess contested on nine
different boards against nine relentless players."

Despite this reputation as a justice whisperer,
Clement's success in his headline cases has been
mixed, a testament to how thorny the issues he's
dealt with are. The 9/11 cases he took on forced
the court and the country to reexamine rules
about executive-branch prerogatives
dating to World War II and think
about what due process meant in
the context of a new kind of conflict.

Clement's preparation for a life
lived in front of the Supreme Court,
he says, began with the "unique
advantages of Georgetown." As a
sophomore, the devout Catholic

'JUSTICE
WHISPERER'
*The former Solicitor
General, now in
private practice, has
argued nearly 100
cases before the
Supreme Court.*

from Milwaukee's suburbs took an internship with his home-state U.S. Senator Bob Kasten. That led to another internship at the White House—"an incredibly heady experience for a 21-year-old," Clement recalls.

Clement's introduction to Washington coincided with a conservative turn at the Supreme Court as President Reagan named William Rehnquist Chief Justice the same year that Antonin Scalia joined the court. A year before Clement arrived on campus, Robert Bork's nomination as an associate justice had been shot down by the Senate Judiciary Committee.

"It caused people to reconsider why they were going to law school," Clement says today. "People were applying with an idea of maybe practicing law at the highest level where it would make a difference."

Not Clement, however. After graduating from the School of Foreign Service summa cum laude in 1988, he continued to entertain notions of finding his way into an international-law practice, continuing his studies at Cambridge University, where he earned a degree in international economics.

It wasn't until after his stint abroad and law school at Harvard, where he served on the law review with Barack Obama, that Clement found himself on a track that would lead him to the podium at the Supreme Court. A clerkship in Washington with Judge Laurence H. Silberman of the U.S. Court of Appeals was followed by one, beginning in 1993, with Justice Scalia himself.

Says Clement: "That's when I got hooked."

> ## "When I got to Georgetown, the people there were talking about all the things they could achieve in their lives."
>
> — DEXTER GOEI (SFS'93)

private practice in 2013) captures how borderless business has become in the 21st century. If the School of Foreign Service was once designed to equip young Americans to manage the country's budding commercial reach abroad, it has had to become a truly cosmopolitan hub, where members of different countries and cultures come together to learn what an integrated global world means in practice.

It was never the intention of Dexter Goei (SFS'93), for instance, to settle and work in the United States. Born in Germany to Indonesian exiles—ethnic Chinese Christians who had fled the strongman Suharto—he grew up, after his parents split, between his mother's home in Paris and his father's home in Los Angeles. In Los Angeles, he gleaned a sense of the American immigrant dream: His father, who had arrived in the United States at age 15, had put himself through college in Michigan by washing dishes at a local restaurant, attended medical school, and become a surgeon. But the real locus of Goei's life was in Paris, where he attended an American school, traveling often to see his grandparents in the Hague. His decision to attend college in the United States was as much aesthetic as it was globalist: Reckoning that he was not Oxbridge material, he rejected his next natural choice, the London School of Economics, when he saw that it "was just a building in the middle of London." He knew that his brother, Danton Goei (SFS'92 and now a portfolio manager in New York), was enjoying Georgetown. Dexter, on a visit, saw that there were plenty of international students besides his brother. "I won't feel as much a foreigner," he recalls thinking.

After graduation, Goei went to work for JP Morgan in Los Angeles, then Morgan Stanley in New York, where he met the telecom entrepreneur Patrick Drahi, the founder of a French cable news channel. Drahi lured his banker, Goei, away from Morgan Stanley to help him expand his business into mobile-phone and internet service, buying up more than 20 companies across Europe and gathering them under the name Altice, a company based in the Netherlands with Goei as CEO. The pair jumped into the American cable market in 2015, buying Suddenlink and Cablevision for a combined $27 billion and spinning it off two years later as Altice USA, which went public in June of 2017.

Professionally, Goei, who now heads the American subsidiary and lives in New York, largely equates Washington with regulations that tend to inhibit his work. Personally, he credits his time in Washington as a student with teaching him about economics, politics, and history, all of which come into play in his current occupation. But the international kid who came to the school because he would feel less foreign has a singular memory of learning to think differently about himself. "When I got to Georgetown, the people there were talking about all the things they could achieve in their lives," he recalls. It was an ambition to find oneself in the world that, despite his global upbringing, he had not encountered elsewhere, and it would drive him to build the international business that he has.

GOOD OPTICS
Dexter Goei with his boss, Altice founder Patrick Drahi, visiting a fiber-network installation team on Long Island, N.Y.

Over There: The Hill Goes to Hollywood

In his short career on campus in 1943, comedian Carl Reiner performed his impressions of School of Foreign Service faculty members, directed a production of Moliere's *A Physician In Spite of Himself*, and took leave to honeymoon with his wife, Estelle, in a rented room on O Street. What he didn't do was get a degree. Enrolled in the Army's Specialized Training Program, Reiner was at Georgetown to study enough French to become a wartime interpreter—and he didn't even accomplish that. After less than a year, he shipped out to the Pacific

with a military entertainment troupe.

Reiner would go on to write for Sid Caesar's *Show of Shows*, create the groundbreaking 1960s hit television series *The Dick van Dyke Show*, and write and direct more than a dozen movies. He did get an honorary Georgetown degree in 2012, at the age of 90. What he shares with the artists who came before and after him on campus is that his Georgetown experience is tied to foreign conflict. War has influenced the School of Foreign Service in many ways, not least in its contributions to the arts.

The first prominent entertainment figure to emerge from the School of Foreign Service was Laurence Stallings (MSFS'22), an imposing former U.S. Marine officer who had fought in the First World War, earning a Silver Star for his actions at Chateau-Thierry in the summer of 1918. While convalescing at Walter Reed Hospital from a wound he suffered at the subsequent Battle of Belleau Wood (which would cost him his leg), Stallings began his novel, *Plumes*. Eventually published to acclaim in1924, after Stallings had gone to work as a reporter for the *New York World* newspaper, it made Stallings's name. King Vidor's silent-film version of the book, *The Big Parade*, came out the next year.

Two years later, Stallings teamed with his *New York World* colleague Maxwell Anderson on *What Price Glory*, a play that portrayed Stallings's wartime experiences in France with a reporter's ear for dialogue and a gritty depiction of war that thrilled Broadway audiences. "For the first time in theatre history," wrote one critic, "a war play was presented with something resembling literal realism, and spoken with more regard for a reasonable verisimilitude than for the sensibilities of convention-protected auditors." The 1926 movie, directed by Raoul Walsh and starring Victor McGlaughlin and Delores del Rio, was another smash hit. Over the next 40 years, until his death in 1968, Stallings would shuttle between New York and Hollywood, writing for the stage and screen, interspersing his play- and screenwriting with assignments as a war correspondent in the

1930s, and, during the Second World War, lending his services as a filmmaker to the Army.

That conflict provided the background for the popular television series *The Rat Patrol*, created by Tom Gries (SFS'44). An Army veteran of the war, Gries began directing movies in the mid-1950s, but by the end of the decade he had turned chiefly to television, directing many episodes of TV Westerns and adventure shows, among them *The Rifleman*, *Route 66*, and *The Man from U.N.C.L.E.* In 1966, Gries came up with the idea of following the exploits of a vanguard of Allied soldiers in dusty jeeps blasting over the desert dunes of the North African campaign. *The Rat Patrol* ran on ABC from 1966 to 1968, before anti-Vietnam War sentiment and strong competition from NBC's *Laugh-In* killed its ratings. Fortuitously, Gries returned to directing movies—most notably *Will Penny*, a 1968 western starring Charlton Heston that is considered the highlight of his career. Gries died in 1977 while finishing his last film, *The Greatest*, a biopic starring its subject, Muhammad Ali.

The Cold War and Vietnam bore artistic fruit, but in disparate ways. Peter Blum (SFS '70), an art dealer who would represent some of the most significant artists of the 1980s and '90s—from Brice Marden to Louise Bourgeois and Alex Katz—got his start as a gallerist working for Galerie Beyeler in Basel, Switzerland, where he'd retreated as a personal protest to the Vietnam War.

Robert Baer (SFS'76) was another critic of the war—while at Georgetown, he remembers, he once climbed onto the roof of Secretary

of Defense Robert McNamara's home during an antiwar march through Georgetown. Yet as a graduate student at the University of California in Berkeley, Baer surprised himself by applying—on a whim, he says—to the CIA. Although disappointed by the intellectual climate at the agency, he nonetheless embarked on a 20-year CIA career, marked largely by his disagreements on tactics. (He was recalled from Iraq in the mid-1990s after unsuccessfully trying to convince his superiors to engage in a plot to overthrow Saddam Hussein.) He left the agency in 1997 and began writing memoirs based on his experiences. His first effort, *See No Evil*, was turned in 2005 into a movie, *Syriana*, starring George Clooney, that leaned heavily on interest in American dealings in the Middle East spurred by the Iraq War that did topple Hussein in 2003.

Hollywood's depiction of the CIA in recent

years as a shadowy force that depends on very human operatives—think *Homeland*—owes something to Baer's alienation and disillusionment as it was shown in *Syriana*. More recently, television shows have portrayed the agency as more competent and more central to the workings of government, thanks in part to shows like NBC's *State of Affairs*, the brainchild of former CIA analyst Rodney Faraon (SFS '92) and Henry Crumpton, Faraon's former CIA colleague and partner in the production company Aardwolf Creative. *State of Affairs*, which ran during the 2014–2015 season, focused on a female CIA agent who is one of the President's daily briefers, a job Faraon knows well. While he never briefed the President himself, he often briefed his former boss—and fellow SFS alum—Bush administration CIA director George Tenet (SFS'76).

BEST WORK
Gries's "Will Penny," starring Charlton Heston.

Chad Griffin

BEFORE HE SAT FOR HIS FIRST CLASS AT Georgetown, Chad Griffin (SFS'97) had worked in the White House, flown on Air Force One, and helped make a Hollywood comedy about the presidency. At the age of 21, fulfilling a promise to his boss, Clinton press secretary Dee Dee Myers, Griffin finally quit politics to finish his college degree, graduating from the School of Foreign Service in 1997.

A native of Bill Clinton's hometown of Hope, Arkansas, Griffin had left his freshman studies at Ouachita Baptist University in Arkadelphia to join Clinton's 1992 run for the Democratic nomination. On Inauguration Day, as the youngest West Wing staffer in history, he watched the Resolute presidential desk replace the C&O desk used by George H.W. Bush.

Equipped with his Georgetown degree, Griffin went to California and reengaged with his political roots. He had gotten to know Rob Reiner, the former *All in the Family* star and film director, while working as the White House liaison to Reiner's *The American President*. Reiner, who was becoming increasingly active in politics in Los Angeles, hired Griffin to help him push through Proposition 10, a ballot initiative that would raise funds for education and child-welfare services by adding a 50-cent tax on every pack of cigarettes sold in the state.

Over the next eight years they followed up, with varying degrees of success, with Proposition 71, supporting stem-cell research, and Proposition 87, aimed at funding alternative energy with taxes on oil.

But it was his efforts against Prop 8, a 2008 ballot initiative, sponsored by a group called Project Marriage, mandating that marriage be defined as a partnership between a man and a woman that established Griffin on the national scene.

While working with Reiner, Griffin had also formed a communications firm with a friend, Kristina Schake, that advertised itself as serving the juncture where Hollywood and politics mixed, representing political Californians like Maria Shriver as well as stars such as Brad Pitt. The firm had been minimally involved in the fight to stop Prop 8, but after the initiative passed in November 2008, Reiner and Griffin decided to wage a legal battle to defeat the measure in the courts. As a vehicle for their campaign, they created the American Foundation for Equal Rights, or AFER.

More important, perhaps, was the legal team Griffin put together in 2010 for the case that would take the Prop 8 question to the Supreme Court. Griffin had heard that Ted Olson, who served as Solicitor General under George W. Bush and had been an avowed opponent of Griffin's former boss, Bill Clinton, supported same-sex marriage. Griffin went to see Olson

STAR POWER
Griffin, right, and opposite with activist Cleve Jones and "Milk" screenwriter Dustin Lance Black in San Francisco's Tenderloin in 2012.

Barack Obama, and his former business partner, Schake, in the same role for the First Lady. Griffin himself was one of the Obama fundraising team's most productive bundlers and had helped lead the charge on liberal causes, from addressing climate change to ending tobacco use.

Yet one year before, Griffin had assumed the presidency of the Human Rights Campaign, one of the country's oldest LGBT advocacy groups and the largest. In his first week at HRC, Griffin publicly criticized Obama for his position on marriage equality, which was to let the states determine their marriage policies individually. Months later, at a gathering at the home of a Hollywood gay couple, he challenged Vice President Joe Biden to speak his mind on same-sex marriage, opening the way for George Stephanopoulos to ask Biden to admit he had no problem with it on *This Week*. Biden obliged by saying he was for it. Days later, Obama said he agreed.

In his seven years leading HRC, Griffin has worked on building grassroots support in places in the United States and abroad where LGBT equality is at its lowest. But Griffin, who announced in late 2018 that he would be leaving HRC, will be best remembered for his opposition to Donald Trump and his promotion of Democratic candidates in the 2018 midterm elections. Whatever the ultimate results of this crusade, which he called "the single largest grassroots expansion in the history of our movement," Griffin showed he could operate as well from the outside as he could as a born insider.

> **At a gathering at the home of a gay Hollywood couple, he challenged Vice President Biden to speak his mind on same-sex marriage, opening the way for Biden to admit he had no problem with it on 'This Week.'**

in Washington and signed him on. Olson in turn brought in liberal superlawyer David Boies. The duo won the case in 2013, laying the foundation for the court's 2015 decision that made same-sex marriage legal in all 50 states.

The day that Prop 8 was defeated, Griffin was still several months shy of turning 40. He was one of the most deeply connected insiders in two of the country's power centers, with his college roommate, Dan Pfeiffer, serving as communications director for then-President

The Media

1. **Kara Swisher** (SFS'84), Co-founder and Editor-at-Large, Recode; 2. **Daniel Henninger** (SFS'68), Deputy Editor of *The Wall Street Journal's* editorial page; 3. **Kate Snow** (MSFS'93), Weekday Anchor for MSNBC Live, National Correspondent for NBC News, Anchor for NBC News Sunday editions; 4. **Kai Ryssdal** (SSP'93), Host of *Marketplace*; 5. **Tania Bryer** (SFS'84), CNBC Host and Executive Producer; 6. **Mark Landler** (SFS'87), White House Correspondent at *The New York Times*; 7. **Tom Sietsema** (SFS'83), Food Critic at *The Washington Post*; 8. **Lulu Garcia Navarro** (SFS'94), Host of NPR's *Weekend Edition Sunday*; 9. **Bob Colacello** (SFS'69), former Editor of *Interview* Magazine, Special Correspondent for *Vanity Fair*; 10. **James Politi** (SFS'99), World Trade Editor for *Financial Times*; 11. **George Crile III** (attended SFS in 1960s), former Producer and Reporter for CBS, Author of *Charlie Wilson's War*; 12. **Shéhérazade Semsar-de Boisséson** (SFS'90, MSFS'90), CEO of *Politico's* European Operation; 13. **Anthony Thomopoulos** (SFS'59), former President of ABC Broadcast Group, former President of United Artists Motion Picture and Television Group; 14. **Justin B. Smith** (SFS'91), CEO of Bloomberg Media Group

07

08

09

12

10

13

11

14

PG 4 photograph by Phil Humnicky, **PG 7** photograph courtesy of Historic American Buildings Survey/Library of Congress, **PG 8** photograph courtesy of Madeleine Albright; **PG 11** photograph by PA Images/Alamy; **PG 12** photograph by US Department of State; **PG 15** photograph by Bettmann/Getty Images; **PG 18** top photograph by 506 collection/Alamy, bottom photograph courtesy of Maria Eitel; **PG 20** top left photograph courtesy of Library of Congress, top right photograph courtesy of U. S. Information Service/Harry S. Truman Library, bottom left photograph by Georgetown University News Service; **PG 21** top photograph courtesy of the United States Trade Representative, bottom right photograph from Ling Lang SFS Courier Vol IV-V; **PG 22** top left photograph from 1962 Georgetown University Record, top right photograph from Georgetown University News Service; **PG 23** top left photograph by Keystone Press/Alamy; **PG 24** bottom left photograph by Photo 12/Alamy; **PG 25** bottom left photograph by Richard Ellis/Alamy, bottom right photograph courtesy of Andrew Shoyer; **PG 26** top left photograph by Scott J. Ferrell/Alamy

Chapter One

PG 29 photograph from AJCU Photographs Collection/Georgetown; **PG 30** photograph from AJCU Photographs Collection/Georgetown University News Service; **PG 31** photograph courtesy of Delta Phi Epsilon; **PG 32** lease courtesy of Delta Phi Epsilon; **PG 33** photograph by Harris & Ewing/Library of Congress; **PG 39** photograph by Leonard Mccombe/Getty Images; **PG 40** MacElwee by Bain Collection/Library of Congress; **PG 43** photograph by National Photo Company Collection/Library of Congress; **PG 47** photograph courtesy of Will J Clinton Presidential Library/National Archives; **PG 49** photograph courtesy of the United States Trade Representative Office; **PG 50** photograph courtesy of Library of Congress; **PG 55** photograph courtesy of OOCL; PG 56 photograph courtesy of Georgetown University; **PG 59** photograph courtesy of United States Holocaust Memorial Museum by Carol Harrison; **PG 60** photograph courtesy of Victoria Espinel; **PG 62** photograph of Komsic courtesy of The White House, photograph of Clinton courtesy of Library of Congress,

photograph of Arias by Frank Scherschel/Getty Images, photograph of Macapagal-Arroyo courtesy US Marines, photograph of Plaza courtesy of US National Archives; **PG 63** photograph of His Majesty King Abdullah II bin al-Hussein by Marvin Nauman/FEMA, photograph of Grybauskaitė courtesy of State Department, photograph of His Majesty King Felipe VI by Generalitat de Catalunya/Wikimedia Commons; **PG 64** photograph of MacElwee courtesy of Library of Congress, remaining photographs courtesy of Georgetown University, **PG 65** photographs courtesy of Georgetown University; **PG 66** photographs courtesy of Georgetown University

Chapter Two

PG 72 photograph courtesy of Library of Congress; **PG 73** photograph courtesy of Library of Congress; **PG 74** by David M/Wikimedia Commons; **PG 81** photograph courtesy of Library of Congress; **PG 86** photograph by Jimmie Taylor/United States Holocaust Memorial Museum/National Archives; **PG 88** photograph courtesy of John F Kennedy Library; **PG 90** photograph by US Department of State; **PG 91** photograph courtesy of Michele Rigby Assad; **PG 98** photograph of Degn by Johannes Jansson/Wikimedia Commons, photograph of Manuel Barroso by 360b/Alamy; photograph of Stoltenberg by paparazzza/Shutterstock, photograph of Collins courtesy of Royal Roads University, photograph of Konfourou by M Stan Reaves/REX, photograph of Mahajan by David Talukdar/Alamy, photograph of Al-Oraibi by Dominic Dudley/Alamy, photograph of Gaviria Trujillo by Allstar Picture Library/Alamy, **PG 99** photograph of Hayden courtesy by the Department of Defense, photograph of Dañino Courtesy of Open Society Foundations, photograph of Zerkal by home for heroes/Shutterstock, photograph of Mohieldin by Luiz Rampelotto/Alamy; **PG 100** photograph of Kono by Kim Stallknecht/Wikimedia Commons, photograph of Ambassador Piromya courtesy of Wikimedia Commons, photograph of Lin courtesy of Wikimedia Commons, photograph of Nielsen by Matthew T. Harmon/United States Department of Homeland Security, photograph of H.H. Sheikh Abdullah bin Hamad Al-Thani by Planetpix/Alamy, photograph of Judeh by Lawrence Jackson/White House, photograph of Ambassador

Stagno Ugarte courtesy of Bruno Stagno Ugarte, photograph of Yi by US Department of State; **PG 101** photograph of White courtesy of B Joseph White, photograph of Spar courtesy of Debora Spar, photograph of Henderson courtesy of Kaya Henderson, photograph of Twillie Ambar by Jason Smith//Alamy, photograph of Biondi courtesy of Saint Louis University

Chapter Three

PG 102 photograph by Peter Turnley/Getty Images; **PG 104** photograph by Army Signal Corps; **PG 105** photograph by New York World-Telegram and the Sun/Library of Congress; **PG 106** photographs courtesy of Robert Rossow III; **PG 109** photograph by SPUTNIK/Alamy; **PG 111** photograph by Sueddeutsche Zeitung Photo/Alamy; **PG 112** photograph courtesy of Library of Congress; **PG 115** photograph Courtesy Gerald R. Ford Library; **PG 116** photograph by Everett Collection Historical/Alamy; **PG 119** photograph by IPA/WENN/Alamy; **PG 125** photograph by Keystone Press/Alamy; **PG 126** photographs courtesy of USAID; **PG 127** photograph courtesy of USAID; **PG 128** photograph courtesy of USAID; **PG 129** photograph by US Marines Photo/Alamy; **PG 130** photograph by Keystone Press/Alamy; **PG 133** photograph courtesy of Mark Medish; **PG 134** photograph by Phil Humnicky/Georgetown University; **PG 136-141** photographs courtesy of Edmund A. Walsh, SJ papers/Georgetown University Library Booth Family Center for Special Collections; **PG 142-143** photographs by the US Department of Defense

Chapter Four

PG 146 photograph by Agencja Fotograficzna Caro/Alamy; **PG 147** photograph by AB Forces News Collection/Alamy; **PG 148** photograph by Boitano Photography/Alamy; **PG 149** photograph by Ami Vitale/Alamy; **PG 150-151** photographs courtesy of Sarah Margon; **PG 152** photograph courtesy of Robert Gallucci; **PG 153** photograph by Georgetown University; **PG 155** photograph by Kim Haughton/UN Photo; **PG 156-157** photographs courtesy of Stephen Cashin; **PG 158** photograph by Everett Collection Historical/Alamy; **PG 159** photograph by White House Photo/Alamy; **PG 160-161** photographs courtesy of David Weiss; **PG 162** photograph courtesy of Mark Yarnell; **PG 164** photograph by USDA

Photo/Alamy; **PG 167** photograph by Jared Platt; **PG 168** photograph by Pete Souza/White House; **PG 170-171** photographs of Sandager, Bauman, Sharp, Durbin, Schuette, Fortuno, Nye, and Mulvaney courtesy of Collection of the US House of Representatives, photograph of Wiliams courtesy of US Senate Historical Office

Chapter Five

PG 172 photograph courtesy of Dexter Goei; **PG 174** photograph by Rebecca J. Moat/US Navy/Alamy; **PG 175** photograph by PJF Military Collection/Alamy; **PG 177** photograph courtesy of Mark Simakovsky; **PG 179** photograph by Jeff McEvoy/US Senate; **PG 180** photograph courtesy of Mark Simakovsky; **PG 181** photograph by Erin A. Kirk-Cuomo/Department of Defense; **PG 184** photograph courtesy of Cheryl Long; **PG 186** photograph by US Army/Interim Archives/Getty Images; **PG 187** photograph of Eisenhower courtesy of Library of Congress; **PG 188-189** photographs courtesy of Philip Verveer; **PG 193** photograph courtesy of Philip Verveer; **PG 195** photograph by Department of Justice; **PG 196** photograph courtesy of Dexter Goei; **PG 198** photograph of The Big Parade Entertainment Pictures/Alamy; **PG 199** photograph by AF archive/Alamy; **PG 200** photograph by Collection Christophel/Alamy; **PG 201** photograph of Baer by Jeff Hutchens/Getty Images, photograph of Will Penny by Moviestore collection Ltd/Alamy; **PG 202** photograph by Matt McClain; **PG 203** photograph by ZUMA Press, Inc./Alamy; **PG 204** photograph of Swisher by Ron Adar/Alamy; photograph of Henninger courtesy of Dan Henninger, photograph of Snow courtesy of Kate Snow, photograph of Ryssdal courtesy of Kai Ryssdal, photograph of Bryer courtesy of Tania Bryer, photograph of Landler courtesy of Mark Landler; **PG 205** photograph of Sietsema courtesy of Tom Sietsema, photograph of Garcia-Navarro by Stephen Voss/NPR, photograph of Colacello by Steve Mack/Alamy, photograph of Semsar-de Boisséson courtesy of Shéhérazade Semsar-de Boisséson, photograph of Thomopoulos by Ron Galella, Ltd/Getty Images, photograph of Smith courtesy of Bloomberg.

ALL UNCREDITED IMAGES courtesy of Georgetown and Georgetown's Booth Center of Special Collections

INTO THE FUTURE
An image from a 1953 yearbook featuring gates on the first floor corridor in Healy Hall, where the School of Foreign Service administrative offices were housed before the Walsh Building opened in 1958. The metal gates survived into the future and still stand in Healy Hall today.

Acknowledgements

The creation of this book would not have been possible without the experiences and stories of all of the people who have been part of the Walsh School of Foreign Service's community since 1919, and especially not without the help of the following groups and individuals:

THE SFS TEAM
Madeleine Albright, Author of the Foreword, Former U.S. Secretary of State and Mortara Endowed Distinguished Professor in the Practice of Diplomacy
Joel S. Hellman, Author of the Introduction, Dean of Georgetown Walsh School of Foreign Service

Will Layman, Executive Director of the Centennial
Jen Lennon, Director of Communications at the Walsh School of Foreign Service
Ara Friedman, Editorial Manager at the Walsh School of Foreign Service
Lynn Conway, University Archivist
Student Researchers and Writers: Percy Metcalfe, Margaux Fontaine, Parker Houston and Nicholas Gavio

THE WASHINGTONIAN CUSTOM MEDIA TEAM
James Byles, President and Publisher
Paul O'Donnell, Writer
Ken DeCell, Editor
Michael Bessire, Design
Kelci Schuler, Photo Editor
Cathy Dobos, Rina Huang and George Perikles, Production Team
Sophia Pizzi and Rebecca Walker, Communications

We are grateful to everyone who has helped with research, photos, design, editing and writing for the pages of this book.